The History of
Newgate Prison

The History of
Newgate Prison

Caroline Jowett

PEN & SWORD
HISTORY

First published in Great Britain in 2017 by
PEN & SWORD HISTORY
an imprint of
Pen & Sword Books Ltd,
47 Church Street,
Barnsley,
South Yorkshire.
S70 2AS

A CIP record for this book is available from the British Library.

ISBN 978 1 47387 640 8

Printed and bound by Gutenberg Press Ltd., Malta

Pen & Sword Books Ltd incorporates the Imprints of
Pen & Sword Aviation, Pen & Sword Maritime,
Pen & Sword Military, Wharncliffe Local History, Pen & Sword Select, Pen &
Sword Military Classics and Leo Cooper.

For a complete list of Pen & Sword titles please contact
Pen & Sword Books Limited
47 Church Street, Barnsley, South Yorkshire, S70 2AS, England
E-mail: enquiries@pen-and-sword.co.uk
Website: www.pen-and-sword.co.uk

Contents

About The Author

Caroline Jowett is an author and arts journalist. She has lived in London for thirty years and is passionate about history, particularly the eighteenth century. She is working on two other books, one non-fiction and the other a novel, and is the former Arts and Books Editor of the *Daily Express*.

Acknowledgements

In the course of writing this book I have drawn not only on original sources, but also on the work of previous historians both in print and online and I owe them debt of gratitude for making my life so much easier, in particular Anthony Babington and Stephen Halliday. Dr Christine Winter's incredibly helpful thesis *Prisons And Punishments In Late Medieval London* gave me a comprehensive understanding of Newgate at that period which would have taken much longer to reach on my own.

If I have managed to give a flavour of how Newgate was for the average inmate, then I should thank professors Jerry White of the University of London and Tim Hitchcock from the University of Sussex whose ability to capture the irrepressible spirit of Londoners, particularly in the eighteenth century, made me feel I was actually standing in the crowd. Professor Hitchcock's invaluable project Old Bailey Proceedings Online also gave me access to original case files – all from the comfort of my own home. Nevertheless, I am grateful to the staff at the British Library and the London Metropolitan Archives for their assistance with original materials both in print and online and to the Gutenberg Project for allowing me to reproduce just a fraction of Grose's *Dictionary of the Vulgar Tongue*. While every effort has been made to ensure accuracy and acknowledge sources, errors and omissions do sometimes unintentionally occur, any there are mine alone and I apologise.

Finally, I'd like to thank my family, in particular my mother, and friends including Dr Sara McCluskey and Elizabeth Jones for their enduring support and encouragement, my editors Heather Williams and Carol Trow for their patience and proof-reading expertise and Jonathan Wright of Pen & Sword for commissioning me to write this book in the first place.

Images

All the images in this publication are certified in the Public Domain in the country of origin where the copyright term is the author's life plus 70 years or less, unless otherwise captioned.

Foreword

If most people were asked to name a prison, the chances are that the first names to spring to mind wouldn't be Wandsworth, Strangeways or Holloway, but the Clink, the Marshalsea or Newgate even though they all closed well over a hundred years ago. It is a testament to the role these places played in our national history and culture, as much as it is to their fearsome brutality and appalling conditions.

Of the three, Newgate, the 'hanging' prison, is for obvious reasons the one we remember most, possibly also because it existed the longest and closed the most recently. From its earliest days, it was the place of incarceration for the most violent prisoners and the place from which thousands set out on the one-way trip to the gallows. It was also, although privately run, the first 'national' gaol, since prisoners from all over the country were held there while awaiting trial.

With apologies to Dickens, Newgate held the best of crimes and the worst of crimes - that is prisoners of conscience, and those who held the establishment to account by annoying parliament and the king, as well as murderers, rapists and arsonists. It housed Ben Jonson and Captain Kidd and myriad men and women who are still household names today. Behind the gatehouse grilles of the medieval prison and the high fortress walls of its eighteenth-century reincarnation was a closed-off world of racketeering and inequality, cruelty and deprivation. Its noisome stink was so terrible by the eighteenth century that, in summer, the shops nearby would be forced to close. In the nineteenth century, it was the focus of reform and by the beginning of the twentieth century it was obsolete.

But this is much more than the story of a prison. It is the story of the development of an entire penal system and perhaps that is another reason why it fascinates us even now, a hundred years after its demolition. To follow the development and changes at Newgate over the 700 years of its existence, is to understand the development of our prison system from the Norman Conquest to the present day. It takes in the shameful practice of transportation and the horror of public execution; the revolutionary concept of a fortress prison and the much needed reorganisation of the whole iniquitous process. The introduction of the enlightened ideas that caused its demise still underpin our thinking today. It is a story of tremendous cruelty and suffering but also of immense compassion, those small acts of kindness that are all one human being can offer another in the face of a brutal regime.

More than any other prison, Newgate has inspired writers and artists. It is largely due to Charles Dickens that even if you have never read *Barnaby Rudge* or *Great Expectations*, Newgate is likely to be the first answer you would give to the question above. It also inspired Daniel Defoe and William Makepeace Thackeray; John Gay set his controversial work *The Beggar's Opera* there and the William Hogarth depicted a hanging outside the gaol in *The Idle 'Prentice* and it continues to draw us today.

If it seems as though nothing much changes in terms of prisoner treatment over the first 450 years of Newgate's existence, it's because nothing much did. Though attempts were made to improve their lot there was a limit to what could be achieved at a time when cruelty, filth, disease, drunkenness, destitution and overcrowding were not confined within the walls of a gaol. It was only when the reformers John Howard and Elizabeth Fry started their campaigns in the eighteenth and nineteenth centuries that things started to change radically. Otherwise it is a litany of the same old complaints followed by the same old solutions. It was not that, within the context of their age, people were deliberately unkind or unthinking. Some were, but there are also plenty of examples where the authorities and officials attempted to mitigate conditions within the gaol, but because of the filth and the threat of disease, they rarely went to check up to see if their orders were being carried out. And of course money was, as it always is, an issue.

It should also be borne in mind that all that has come down to us are the very worst cases and practices. No one records the minor offenders, the petty injustices, the innocent, the well-behaved and, on the whole, no one records the poor unless they have committed a crime. In among the cases mentioned will be thousands of others who lived, and maybe died, unremarked and unaccounted for within Newgate's walls, sometimes without even a name.

The gaol was demolished in 1904 to make way for a super-improved Central Criminal Court of the Old Bailey, still the place where the nation's most heinous crimes, including murder, are heard. Only a wall in Amen Corner, a door in the Museum of London and a couple of condemned cells in the basement of a pub across the street remain, but Newgate's ghost lingers on.

Caroline Jowett, London, 2016

Chapter 1
Foundations
1188 - 1499

LONDON BEFORE NEWGATE

London in the Middle Ages was still the walled city it had been since Roman times. Southwark and Westminster, the two other communities that over the centuries would merge with it and expand to form the London we know today, were no more than villages. Southwark, a haven of criminals and unregulated trade on the south, Surrey, side of the Thames, was the home of St Thomas's Hospital and later that notorious den of lawlessness the Southwark Mint. Westminster, on the other hand, with its royal palace and abbey was the seat of government. Like the City, Westminster was on the north, Middlesex, side and the two settlements were connected by the single straight line of Fleet Street and The Strand. In common with the City, Southwark and Westminster had their own sheriffs, courts and gaols.

The City walls had seven gates: Ludgate, Newgate, Moorgate, Cripplegate, Bishopsgate, Aldersgate and Aldgate through which ran the main roads to other parts of the country. The road that passed through Newgate ran to the south and west to Reading, Dorset and Hampshire. If necessary, for example in times of rebellion and therefore high arrest rates, when London's two official prisons were full, these gatehouses would be pressed into use.

By the middle of the twelfth century, the two official prisons were the Tower of London, and the Fleet. Both had been built shortly after the Norman Conquest and were under the jurisdiction of the king. Outside London, justice was in the hands of the nobles and prison was the dungeon or keep of the local lord's castle, where the idea of incarceration as a punishment in itself did not exist. Gaol was more like a remand centre of today, though nowhere near as comfortable, where prisoners would be held pending trial. Nor was there was any segregation of prisoners either by sex or crime, women and men, murderers and pickpockets were all jumbled in together.

The Tower, as is often thought, was not exclusively for the use of nobles who had got on the wrong side of the king but was open to anyone who fell foul of the law. The Fleet, which before the construction of Newgate was known as the Gaol of London, also housed felons (serious offenders), committers of misdemeanours (petty offenders) and debtors. Like modern prisons they were built on the edge of the community, the Tower to the east on the Thames south of Aldgate and the Fleet by the river Fleet that flowed into the Thames at Ludgate in the west. But they were close enough to the gates to serve as a daily reminder, in the days before a police force, of the need to obey the law. They were the first purpose-built prisons in the country and today only the Tower remains.

BUILDING NEWGATE

In 1188, Henry II, an enthusiastic if occasionally ruthless reformer who laid the foundations of English Common Law and our jury system, decreed that London needed another prison. It would be under the administration of the City of London itself, a first, though Henry, would make occasional grants and also keep a watching brief to ensure the authorities were doing their job properly. A piece of land next to Newgate where Newgate Street joined Old Bailey was purchased for £3 6s 8d, two carpenters and a smith were hired and the new prison built. Given the occupations of the builders it seems probable that, unlike the Tower and the Fleet, this first Newgate was made of wood.

In 1236, the City and the Crown funded some improvements to the tune of £100 and one of the gatehouse's stone turrets and the dungeons were incorporated into the gaol. Even at this early stage, prisons were divided into a masters and a common side, for rich and poor so when in 1281-2 the privy was cleaned and the 'aperture in the stone wall for ejecting excrement' was mended as part of a wider programme of repairs costing £66, it is probable that this was on the masters side. It is unlikely that the common side would have enjoyed such fancy sanitation arrangements.

In addition, the ditches and sewers were cleared, two windows installed and two doors created between the prisoners and the privy. The prisoners remained on site during the repairs and four extra guards were hired for four nights to prevent escapes. After that, nothing much was done for 200 years except that in 1316, Edward II ordered that the sewer, which was in a very bad state, should be 'restored at speed'.

In 1406, a group of female prisoners complained about their cramped accommodation and that to reach the privy, they had 'to their great shame and hurt' to go through the men's quarters. A separate tower was built for them, though it probably amounted to them having their own sleeping quarters since the idea of the segregation of men and women was still a long way off and there was free movement within the gaol. There is evidence of women getting pregnant while in Newgate, though whether this was non-consensual or a way of passing the time is impossible to tell. Women could escape a hanging if they were pregnant by 'pleading the belly', so it might have been a mixture of all three.

By now, Newgate was far from the most recent addition to London's proto-penal system. Nine other gaols had been added since the end of the twelfth century, making a total, including the Fleet and the Tower, of twelve. There was a new gaol five minutes down the road at Ludgate while The Tun, so-called because of its barrel shape, was on Cornhill and mostly housed 'street walkers and lewd women'. There were two compters, a cross between a prison and a sheriff's office, at Bread St and Poultry St, which held debtors, adulteresses and minor offenders. Until these new gaols were introduced, sheriffs had held and tried people in their own homes.

The compters, The Tun, Ludgate and Newgate were administered by the City. Under the Crown's control were: the Marshalsea of the Household and the Marshalsea of the King's Bench in Southwark which held, among others, men accused of crimes at sea, those convicted of sedition and of course the ubiquitous debtors. The Clink, on the notorious Bankside where brothels, theatres and a colourful nightlife flourished, was under the jurisdiction of the Bishop of Winchester and it held anyone who broke his rules. In addition, there were stocks and pillories placed on the busiest thoroughfares and market squares since public humiliation played a big part in the medieval concept of punishment.

In 1419, it was decided that the gaol at Ludgate, which had been operational for about a hundred years, should close and all the prisoners transferred to Newgate. This led to such terrible overcrowding that within months there was a sharp spike in deaths blamed on Newgate's 'fetid and corrupt atmosphere' and Ludgate was re-opened.

By now Newgate was 250 years old, and although some parts were considerably newer, some, for example, the dungeons, might have been even older and overall the gaol was in a pretty appalling condition. It seems that the Lord Mayor, Richard Whittington, thought so at any rate because in 1423 he left money in his will for it to be completely rebuilt.

The new gatehouse and gaol was on a much bigger and grander scale than its predecessor and took around eight years to build. While construction was going on the prisoners were sent to the Bread Street Compter up the road at Cheapside. The new gaol arched over Newgate Street and stretched down Old Bailey, and it reflected changes in prisoner management that had evolved since it was founded.

It housed 150 inmates, with separate quarters for men and women, and minor criminals were to be kept apart from serious offenders though this was loosely adhered to at best. This indicates a desire to improve conditions for the poorest inmates. There was a hall, a chapel, day and night wards, privies, underground dungeons and rooms with chimneys. It also had a water fountain, which was impure and made the inmates very ill. Over the centuries, Newgate's terrible stench became legendary, almost a living inmate of the prison in its own right. After the gaol's demolition in 1904, an underground waterway was discovered which might have been the source of the smell and this fountain of bad water.

Among the improvements was a fresh water supply from St Bartholomew's

Hospital, installed shortly after the prison was finished, maybe after the authorities discovered the water in the fountain was undrinkable. Later, a former Lord Mayor, Thomas Knollys paid for lead pipes to be installed to provide more fresh water and clean the privy. He was also granted a licence to supply water to the poor prisoners of Newgate and Ludgate so the fountain may just have been intended for those on the masters side.

This new gaol became known among thieves as the Whittington, more commonly shortened to the Whit, and lasted with only minor alterations until 1666, when it was badly damaged in the Great Fire and extensively repaired.

CONDITIONS

While there was no real segregation of prisoners according to gender or offence, there was clear segregation based on wealth; money talked and even those convicted of the most serious crimes could buy themselves luxury and comfort until their case came up.

Gaols were privately run and the accused had to fund their own stay. Even before Whittington's Newgate was built, it seems that gaols were divided into a masters side, where experience of prison life could be vastly improved according to ability to pay, and a common side, where the poor man's experience would be one of unrelenting squalor and almost unimaginable misery. There were some exemptions to fees: the destitute who relied on alms, and anyone committed by the mayor, aldermen or sheriffs, these were exempt from the committal and deliverance fees and also from the payment to maintain the lamps in the corridors which was 4d unless provided by charity.

Though the terms masters and common were not used until much later it is clear that even from its earliest days, there were rooms offered out at differing rates and for different categories of prisoner.

An ordinance issued in 1431, as Whittington's gaol was completed, allocated the accommodation with the areas surrounding the gate housing 'freeman of the City and other honest persons' – men to the north and women to the south. These were the best rooms and would have probably had windows, fireplaces and chimneys. They would have been higher up in the building away from noise and nearer fresh air. Anyone who was not a freeman of the City of London (that is anyone outside the protection of the Livery Companies which governed the trades) or was a stranger to the City would get the next best accommodation. Felons, major offenders and anyone thought to be an escape risk were held in the underground dungeons known as 'holes', which were small, damp and without natural light. Even then, the authorities were aware of the effect of these places on the health of prisoners and of the risk of infection, but either the keepers didn't have anywhere else to put them or they didn't much care.

With the masters side on the upper floors, the poor prisoners of the common

chummage

side had to make do with the lower floors where the smell was thicker, the light dimmer and the air damper. Under a system known as chummage, a prisoner on the masters side might pay a poorer cellmate off and have his or her own room, or maybe share with one other person, a 'chum', while on the common side prisoners were herded into wards where there was no privacy at all. Prisoners could also pay either to have a lighter set of irons fitted or escape ironing altogether. This was called easement of irons and didn't stop until the end of the eighteenth century.

In the new Whittington-financed Newgate of the mid-fifteenth century, the keeper was forbidden from charging freemen and freewomen prisoners more than a penny a night for a bed with a blanket and sheets or a penny a week for the use of a couch. If the inmates wanted to bring their own beds from home, they could do so for free. Bed and board for a gentleman or freeman was 3s a week, 2s for a yeoman, and the keeper was banned from selling candles, food or charcoal so that prisoners could shop around. Presumably this was an attempt to weaken the keeper's monopoly on goods sold within the prison and stop the perennial complaints of overcharging; whatever the reason, it was not long before the keepers were back in charge of their monopoly.

In the taprooms, prices stayed the same as they had before the gaol was rebuilt, perhaps because the water was still undrinkable. It was a poor deal for the keepers who bought in best ale at 3½d a gallon but were only allowed to sell it on for tuppence. Unless they could sell it to visitors at an inflated price, they would have lost money.

The fees for coal were 2d a bushel, 1d a half bushel and ½d a peck 'full and heaped up'. A bushel and a peck were imperial dry measures of goods. A bushel was eight gallons (about 36.5 litres) and a peck two gallons (nine litres).

Garnish was payable on entry to the prison but was due to the cellarman not the prison authorities. The intention was that it would provide extras such as clean straw, more candles, beer and blankets or to provide charity for those who were too poor to fund themselves. However, it was frequently abused and often the cellarman would drink it away. Garnish had to be paid and there was no comeback against unscrupulous cellarmen as the authorities turned a blind eye to the whole practice. This wasn't so hard on the masters side where inmates could afford to purchase whatever they needed, but on the common side it might mean sitting in the dark, sleeping on the bare floor or having nothing to eat. Prisoners who couldn't pay had to forfeit their clothes and the cry on entry to the ward was 'pay or strip'.

At the King's prisons, such as the Fleet, inmates were sometimes allowed to leave on licence to carry on their businesses or sort out personal affairs, and it is possible this also applied to the City-regulated Newgate. They could also make articles for sale. At the end of the fifteenth century, for example, a haberdasher called John Wysbeche provided bones for the prisoners to carve which he then sold. If they didn't get money in exchange for this work, it is likely they would have received food or other preferential treatment. There is evidence that this practice carried on throughout Newgate's history. At the end of the eighteenth century one inmate did a roaring trade in hand-made artificial flowers.

With poor sanitation in the gaol, diseases such as cholera were rife. It is impossible to determine how many people died from sickness or starvation in the early years of the prison's existence since records are patchy. However, there is a twenty-seven-year period at the beginning of the fourteenth century where 549 deaths were recorded in the City. Of these, 190, just over a third, died in prison and of those between 1315 and 1340, 160 were in Newgate, eleven in the Tower and nineteen over the river in the Marshalsea. Many of these were recorded as 'rightful death' - that is not from disease or starvation but, in the absence of forensics and pathology, natural causes. Surprisingly, none appear to be the result of violence.

The biggest fear among the prisoners and the biggest problem for the officials right up to the nineteenth century was gaol fever, also known as crinkums. It's now recognised as a form of typhus known as *Rickettsia prowazekii*, but in the Middle Ages it was thought to be an unpreventable condition of prison life. It thrives in overcrowded, poorly-sanitised conditions such as gaols and slums and is carried by lice. There are accounts of prisoners being so swarmed with these vermin that their clothes seemed to move of their own accord and the floor of Newgate was so covered in them that their bodies cracked beneath the feet of anyone crossing the floor.

The bites itch and when they are scratched with filthy fingers they become infected with dirt and faeces and the disease takes hold. Symptoms include a rash, nausea, vomiting - enough to bring up blood - retching, tremors, headaches and purple lesions on chest and back, weakness, thirst, chest pains and convulsions. It is extremely virulent and in the cramped conditions of a prison can spread like wildfire through wards and down corridors. Perversely, sometimes only one person would be infected. In 1419, gaol fever killed the keeper and sixty-four inmates and in 1750, a group of prisoners brought it into the Old Bailey sessions house when they came for trial and it killed another sixty-four including the Lord Mayor.

If a prisoner had no money or means of support, or were so old or ill they were likely to die, the king, the mayor and aldermen could authorise a release.

On the common side, the food ration was a penny loaf a day, that is a small loaf weighing about 8oz (228g), sometimes made of pure ingredients, sometimes packed with alum or other cheap flour substitutes. To supplement this, the inmates relied on alms, confiscated goods and the leftovers from rich men's tables and records show they had a reasonably regular supply of food and drink which would have sustained them, even if it did not make them fat.

Sometimes these were one-off donations; for example William Halyot left orders in his will for two oxen to be distributed round London's prisons. Newgate and Ludgate got half an ox each, while the rest got smaller portions.

Excavations on the site of the Fleet prison give an indication of what the Newgate prisoners' diet might have been - it would not have varied much over the centuries and could have included blackberries, cherries, elderberries, hazelnuts, grapes, plums and sloes, which were grown in the grounds of the Fleet, as well as mulberries and figs. Vegetable seeds found included Brussels sprouts, cabbage, cauliflower, kale, swede and turnip while cereals included barley, club wheat, hemp and oats and even opium poppy.

In terms of meat and fish, there is evidence their diet would have included beef, chicken, deer, duck, goose, lamb, pork, rabbit, teal and woodcock, eel, flounder, hake, herring, plaice and smelt.

It is likely the keeper had arrangements with the local shopkeepers for the supply of produce that he could then sell onto his charges, though it is also possible that the prisoners grew some of their own food. An ordinance of 1431 banning keepers from monopolising the sale of food suggests they were doing just that, and complaints about the exorbitant charges echo down the centuries.

In the religious Middle Ages, good deeds were important as it was believed they were a means of getting to Heaven, though it is also true to say that the charity was given more for the benefit of the giver, who was hoping to store up reward points in the next world, than for the benefit of the needy in this. In the Seven Acts of Mercy, visiting prisoners and giving alms were two steps laid down by the Church on the stairway to Heaven, so donations of money, wine and food poured into the City's gaols. In 1237, Sir John Poultry, a draper and former Lord Mayor, gave a small annuity for the use of prisoners in Newgate and in 1385, the serving Lord Mayor did the same thing. Another benefactor asked for 'a cad of good red herring' to be supplied every Lent to the poorest prisoners of Newgate, Ludgate, the King's Bench and the Marshalsea. There were also bequests such as Dick Whittington's, though they weren't all generous enough to fund the rebuilding of a gaol. Some paid for the provision of meat on Sundays and others for a supply of clean water. It wasn't just individuals who donated; manufacturers, tradesmen and livery companies also made donations and in 1303 one livery company ordered that the remains of its feasts should be given to the poor Newgate prisoners.

The poorest prisoners often begged through the gate and the grilles of the gaol using long spoons with deep bowls to enable them to reach further into the street. Competition for a place here was fierce and, it seems, caused a nuisance to anyone passing under Newgate's arch; passers-by would walk in the middle of the road to avoid their pockets being picked.

In 1431, the Court of Aldermen put the begging on an official footing and allowed two pairs of prisoners, accompanied by a turnkey, to beg, one down by the river, the other within the City centre. To identify them as coming from Newgate each pair carried a sealed box and a saucer with the gaol's name printed on them. The boxes were opened by the sheriffs at the end of each month, and the contents used to help the penniless inmates.

Anyone found selling goods in contravention of the City's strict trading regulations could have these confiscated and given to the prisoners at Newgate and other City gaols. In the 1320s, bakers were found to be selling underweight bread and there are many instances where meat considered unfit for sale was passed on to the 'lucky' prisoners. In another incident, bakers bypassed the City's wheat supplier at Bridge House and bought their grain more cheaply from an unauthorised source. The wheat sold at Bridge House carried a tax, which was earmarked for the rebuilding of London Bridge; by purchasing their wheat from an unregulated supplier the bakers were avoiding the tax and the authorities took a dim view of anyone whose actions went against the wider interests of the community. When they were caught the bakers forfeited their loaves to Newgate.

ADMINISTRATION

While the Tower of London and the Fleet were the King's prisons, Newgate was the responsibility of the City of London. The Lord Mayor was the chief magistrate who judged and sentenced the inmates. He also presided over the Court of Aldermen. These twenty-six men were also members of, and responsible to, London's legislative body, the Court of Common Council and the Crown. They also set down the rules by which Newgate operated, oversaw its maintenance and repair, kept an eye the conditions and dispensed justice.

Like all bureaucrats, it seems they were very good at issuing ordinances and regulations but less good at following up to see if they were being obeyed. Or maybe, since it seems they took their responsibilities very seriously and tried to curb the worst of the cruelty, the way to best manage prisoners was as much of a head-scratching issue as it is today. Over the centuries, their ordinances repeatedly cover the same issues: poor conditions; cruelty; extortion and bad food, which indicates that they weren't as effective as they might have liked to be. Part of the problem was that no one wanted to visit the prisons to ensure their orders were being carried out. This was partly down to a squeamishness about the filth and the squalor and partly due to a very understandable fear of disease.

Under the Court of Aldermen were the sheriffs who were the legal officials responsible for the arrest, custody and production of the accused for trial. If, as happened in 1258, a prisoner escaped, then the sheriffs and the Lord Mayor would be held responsible. When, in this case, they were called to account, Henry III, freed the mayor, but sent the sheriffs to the Tower for a few months while he recovered his temper. If a prisoner needed bringing to or from Newgate or another gaol, that too was the sheriff's job so the risk of escape was a real one. The responsibility didn't fall wholly on their shoulders though; the Keeper of Newgate had to sign a bond to the sheriffs against his prisoners escaping and any failure in his duty that resulted in an escape was severely punished.

The prisons were in the charge of a keeper who was responsible for the day-to-day running - a thankless, difficult and dangerous job. Sometimes the position was inherited, sometimes given by a patron, but generally, it was put out to tender and sold to the highest bidder. Since the position attracted either a small salary or none at all, the keeper would then set the fees for a whole raft of services from entry to exit, including for food, blankets, and candles, in an attempt to make back the money he had spent on securing the appointment and also to provide himself with an income. Out of his own pocket, he also paid for a staff of turnkeys, the building's maintenance and for keeping it clean. In order to maximise his return, the keeper might be tempted to run his gaol on a shoestring, though there is evidence that others made efforts to maintain standards and others still were granted licences for carts to remove the waste. Nevertheless, it could be extremely lucrative.

Prisoners were also allowed to have food and goods brought in from outside. The cellarmen and corrupt turnkeys were entitled to a cut of this, either in money or in kind. And for those unable to afford the keeper's prices and without friends or family to provide for them, there was charity and confiscated food.

A taproom sold beer and spirits at a price set by the keeper. In 1370 an ordinance banned brewing and baking (indicating access to a kitchen) and selling of food within the gaol, but in 1393 this was amended to allow food to be sold provided it wasn't overpriced.

More often though, these keepers were greedy and cruel and it took around 150 years for it to dawn on the City authorities that the quality of the prisons might be dependent on the quality of the men they appointed to run them. In 1356, as part of sweeping set of reforms to the prison system, it was decreed that the position of Keeper of Newgate could not be sold and it would be the duty of the authorities to appoint a man of appropriate good character. In 1421, this was extended to other City gaols. As part of these reforms, a new set of regulations was also drawn up which, upon taking office, the appointee had to swear to abide by. Among other things, he was banned from charging for the removal of irons, though this was changed in 1393 when a limit of £5 was set. The keeper also had to give surety for the safety of his prisoners, which also included moving them between the City gaols, around the countryside, or to Tyburn the village, near the site of today's Marble Arch, where a gallows stood ready to hang the guilty.

In the 1430s, it was decided that only the most serious offenders would be fettered and the keeper was banned for charging for extras such as beds and candles. The discharge fee was limited to 4d for anyone who wasn't a traitor or a felon. It seems these efforts were well intentioned and to some extent they must have succeeded, since the convictions of keepers for violence to the men and women in their care are surprisingly few. However, the charging of fees and the treatment of prisoners were bones of contention, which, in spite of the appointment of the first prison inspectors in 1463, were wrestled over for centuries, and complaints against the greed and cruelty of the keepers never stopped. Some fell foul of the law themselves, the earliest recorded example being that of John Shep in 1244. Shep, a sergeant to one of the sheriffs, was convicted of causing the death of a prisoner by hurling him violently into the deepest chamber of Newgate and breaking his neck. And in 1290, a Newgate gaoler was hanged for murdering an inmate. Two early fourteenth-century keepers, Edmund de Lorimer and Hugh de Croydon, were convicted of torturing prisoners to extort money. In 1449, the keeper was gaoled, accused of violating a female prisoner. And in 1487, the keeper and his wife were put in Bread St Compter for abusive language and failing to obey a summons. And there was always the possibility of imprisonment and fines for the keeper himself should a prisoner escape or die in his custody.

Heavy fines were also levied against sheriffs and keepers guilty of mistreating their prisoners, suggesting that allegations of cruelty were taken extremely seriously, and the punishment intended to deter further incidences. It should also be remembered that it is only the evidence of maltreatment that has come down to us, and it is possible that among the violent and brutal officials were others who treated their inmates with more compassion.

The violence was not all on the side of the keeper and his turnkeys. From the outset, Newgate held the most violent and desperate criminals, and men facing the death penalty have nothing left to lose, so the keeper and his officers were vulnerable to attack.

Under the keeper were the turnkeys (warders), a steward and his deputy. Since prisons were privately run, and the keepers were generally looking to keep costs down to maximise their profits, gaols were often understaffed and Newgate was no exception. Security was provided by the shackles that were loaded onto the prisoners on arrival, and the worst offenders or those thought most likely to escape, would have theirs bolted to rings or brackets on the walls or floor. In this way, the thrifty keeper could keep his expenditure on turnkeys to a minimum.

The steward and his deputy looked after all the supplies in the prison. Until 1633 this was a salaried position but after that it was decided that the prisoners should elect one of their own number as steward. This step towards self-governance led to the prison-republics of the eighteenth century.

The cellarmen and women were prisoners themselves. Each was elected by his or her peers to run a ward and they collected garnish for the benefit of the ward.

Apart from an historical association with St Sepulchre's opposite Newgate, there was no formal arrangement for the religious welfare of the prisoners until

1544 when a temporary part-time chaplain was appointed. The medical care of the prisoners was in the hands of nearby St Bartholomew's Hospital from its foundation until 1757 when it got its own medical team.

TRIALS

Prisoners committed for trial, who could afford it, could be released on bail or find one or a group of mainpernors to pay a surety against them appearing at court on a specified day. A mainpernor was not dissimilar to a bail guarantor today. In the thirteenth and fourteenth centuries this even applied to pirates and murderers. Acceptance of the surety was at the judge's discretion and there is evidence that occasionally it was accepted but the prisoner was not released. Sometimes bail was refused because the accuser was in cahoots with someone in the legal process, maybe the clerk and, occasionally, a defendant might not even know why they had been committed for trial.

Gaol or prison? The essential difference between a gaol and a prison is that a gaol is for holding prisoners awaiting trial or punishment while a prison is a place of incarceration where the imprisonment is a punishment in itself. The distinction has disappeared in the United Kingdom where today we have custody suites, remand centres and prisons, which are separate from the courts, but it still exists in the United States of America. Newgate was a gaol since it was where prisoners were held before making an appearance at the affiliated sessions house and then, after sentencing, where they waited for their punishment to be carried out, attempted to clear their debts, or raised the fee for their release. Gaol delivery was when all the prisoners were sent for trial. In the early days when there were no regular sessions, this could mean a wait of months or occasionally years, since the sheriffs would wait until the gaol was bursting at the seams before clearing it out. Before the fifteenth century, Newgate was delivered roughly twice a year, which in a gaol with a capacity of 150, probably amounted to much the same thing. One of the sessions was the sheriff's responsibility, the other the Lord Mayor's, but by 1475 there were five sessions a year and, if necessary, the Lord Mayor or the king could intervene and order more. By the eighteenth century, there were eight sessions a year, in an attempt to reduce overcrowding and keep the prison population moving.

Sessions were held in a room inside the prison itself, but this was unpopular with the magistrates who were reluctant to endure the filth and smell and risk of disease. In 1354, Newgate got its own sessions house, next door on Old Bailey. The delivery fee at Newgate before Whittington's rebuilding was 4d, after which it was 8d, except for felons who had to pay 2s.

Oyer et Terminer, from the French meaning 'to hear and determine' was one of the commissions by which assize judges sat. Under it they were required to try cases of treason and felony. *Peine forte et dure* was not so much a punishment as a Catch-22 of barbaric cruelty designed to force the accused to enter a plea. In law, an accused person could not be convicted unless he had already pleaded guilty to the charges before him, but since conviction would result in the automatic confiscation of all his goods and property, prisoners would sometimes exercise a kind of early right to remain silent and refuse to plead. The idea of this was that with no plea, there would be no conviction, and his property would remain with his wife and family. To get round this and in an attempt to 'persuade' him to plead, the law came up with *peine forte et dure*, French for 'strong and hard pain'.

The prisoner would lie naked on the floor and iron weights or block of stone would be piled on his chest until he changed his mind or died. He was allowed only three pieces of bread on one day and three sips of water on the next. If he maintained his refusal to plead - and a few hardy souls did - then he died in the knowledge that his family was provided for. If he gave in and pleaded, then it was up to the judge to rule whether he would stand trial, or be left where he was to die. For obvious reasons, it became known as the 'press' and the prison yard became known as the press yard, though in Whittington's Newgate there was a special room. The last known use of *peine forte et dure* was in 1741; It was abolished in 1772.

If a prisoner had a complaint about the justness of their imprisonment they could either, publicise their plight and hope to drum up support for their cause, or they could appeal directly to the Court of Chancery. There, the Chancellor of England would consider the legality of their case and make a judgment. A prisoner needed money and time to put an appeal together so would-be appellants were usually from the masters side. Appeals were very formulaic and grovelling and were designed to elicit the greatest sympathy for the appellant's plight and win their release. Much of the evidence about conditions at Newgate has come from these accounts, however there are also independent reports which back up the assertions that life inside was appalling. Appeals could also be very expensive. Walter de Guildford claimed £100 in damages to cover the cost of his appeal against a sentence of eighteen days on charges of conspiracy and trespass. The Court of Appeal wasn't introduced until the end of the nineteenth century.

Complaints such as those brought against Edmund de Lorimer and Hugh de Croydon, are not as numerous as one might suppose. Relatively few officials had any of these very serious charges brought against them and so men such as de Lorimer and de Croydon stand out disproportionately. The complaints mentioned earlier against John Shep, and the keeper who was hanged in 1290 for breaking a man's spine after fitting an iron collar too tightly, were fifty years apart. It was another twenty-five years before, in 1314, a prisoner complained that he had been kept in one of the dungeons, tortured and loaded with chains until he agreed to pay de Lorimer a large sum for his release. De Lorimer was sent to the Fleet where presumably he got a taste of his own medicine. A few years after that de Croydon was dismissed for the same crime. So it may be that, while a few may have been truly evil and others were little better than penny-pinching racketeers, some least were, in the context of their time, doing the best they could with violent people under a brutal system.

Chapter 2
Crimes and Punishments
1188 - 1499

HOW TO FIND YOURSELF IN NEWGATE

A term of imprisonment wasn't considered a punishment in itself until the late thirteenth century. The commonest sentence was a year and a day, as in the case of a lawyer who'd deceived the court. In 1361 the sentence for stealing a hawk was two years, which shows the value of a hawk against the truth, and kidnappers got life.

Sometimes however, there could be a long time between arrest and trial. One man petitioned the Prince of Wales and the Lord Mayor because he had been in Newgate for four years awaiting trial, while John de Mundon was in Newgate for five years after the sheriff complained against him in 1352. Both men claimed errors had been made in their committal. Unfortunately, Mundon was not successful on a technicality - he had filled in the form incorrectly - proving that petty bureaucracy was alive and well in fourteenth-century London.

As the most secure gaol in the area, Newgate housed the most serious offenders in London and Middlesex almost from the outset, and it was not long before sheriffs across England and Wales were ordered to send their worst criminals (at the criminal's expense) to Newgate to appear at the Old Bailey sessions house. Murder was unusual in the Middle Ages, theft and debt were the biggest problems, but there were plenty of other felonies and misdemeanours that could land someone in Newgate including assault, burglary and carrying arms in the street. What constituted a crime, then as now, was based very much on actions that were considered to undermine or threaten the society. If someone believed themselves to have been a victim of crime it was up to them to make the case, and for that he required the perennially rare properties of time and money. As a result, many criminals escaped prosecution - though of course they may have faced street justice.

Prisoners learned to play the system against itself by turning informer while vigilantes and thief-takers milked it from the outside. It was not uncommon for 'witnesses' to hang around outside the court offering their 'evidence' to anyone who needed backing up. The were known as men of straw and they usually indicated their presence by pieces of straw stuck in their shoes The king had supreme power over the prisons, so he could manage their populations and would step in and order a gaol delivery if they became too overcrowded.

Felony

Felonies were serious crimes such as murder, burglary and highway robbery, that usually resulted in the confiscation of land and property and the death penalty. Since there was free movement within the gaol and all prisoners were held together regardless of crime, anyone in a gang who'd turned informer and grassed up his mates must have felt more than a bit nervous. Over the life of Newgate prison an inordinate number of cases heard at the Old Bailey sessions house related to property.

Misdemeanours

Misdemeanours still exist under English law. Generally, they are less serious than felonies and carry a lighter sentence, for example, a fine. Early courts liked to hit people where it hurt. Examples of misdemeanours include being drunk and disorderly, brawling, trespass and prostitution. Those committing misdemeanours probably found themselves in Newgate because it was the most convenient prison at the time of arrest. Their fine would be set to reflect the severity of the offence. So thumping someone would result in a fine of half a mark, but drawing blood was twenty shillings. Likewise using a dagger to threaten a victim during a robbery might get fifteen days, but using it to draw blood would carry a sentence of, maybe, forty.

Definitions of misdemeanours and their appropriate punishments were set down by the City authorities, which were responsible for maintaining law and order and protecting their citizens. Attacks on the City's authority were taken particularly seriously.

At the end of the thirteenth century, assault cases were also generally settled on payment of a fine, though assaults on City officials attracted a harsher penalty, usually involving imprisonment.

In 1380 two men were caught pretending to be mutes and begging even though 'they were stout enough to work for their food and raiment and had tongues to talk with'. They were detained indefinitely.

And in the mid-fifteenth century, Thomas Derlyng, sergeant to Walter Cottone, sheriff, was sentenced to imprisonment in Newgate and the pillory for slandering John Penne, an alderman. His sentence was upheld as a 'pernicious example... for other false lies against City officials' and he never held public office again.

Debtors

Debtors made up by far the bulk of the prison population. A distinction between debtors and the rest of the prison population began to be drawn at the end of the fourteenth century. Today when we think of debtors' prisons it is through the prism of Dickens and his nineteenth century accounts of the Marshalsea, but by then the reasoning behind imprisonment for debt had been lost in the mists of time. It seems a nonsense today to deprive a person of their liberty, and therefore their chance to earn the money to settle the debt, but by Dickens' time the system had become a travesty. In the Middles Ages, imprisonment for debt was less 'can't pay' and more 'won't pay' and it was one of the ways the Crown could force nobles to settle outstanding debts with the Exchequer - if they paid up they would then be released. By 1352, it had been widened to give redress to private creditors who could imprison a debtor until he paid up, the intention being that his friends and family would rally round to settle the debt, though occasionally a benefactor would step in. As with all other prisoners, a debtor would be expected to keep himself while in gaol, thus adding to his costs, so it wasn't unusual for him to move his whole family in to save on rent. The only exception to this was destitution, when the creditor had to provide enough bread and water to keep his prisoner alive. It was to be another four hundred years before creditors would be obliged to hand over an allowance of 4d a day to keep their debtors.

By this time, it was also established, on agreement and payment of a fee to the keeper, that some debtors could carry on their businesses from the prison; impecunious clergymen would advertise and perform cut-price weddings and christenings, for example, and lawyers on the skids would dispense discounted legal advice. Some people lived like that for years, as the debtor would not be released until the debt was paid or the creditor gave up or died.

Treason

There are two types of treason - high, which relates to extreme acts against a monarch, for example conspiracy, regicide or even, in the eighteenth century, coin-clipping since it devalued the currency thus undermining the economy; and petty which covers certain crimes against a (then) social superior for example murder of a husband by a wife or a master or mistress by a servant. Both carried the death penalty.

It was not just the Tower of London that held prisoners of state. From 1488 Newgate, though not one of the King's prisons, also had its fair share. Political prisoners could be prisoners of war held hostage as part of peace negotiations, or supporters of the king's enemies who could be used to secure a ransom or the return of captives held abroad. Political prisoners would also cover men whose politics annoyed the king. Generally, prisoners of state were housed in accommodation befitting their status and were allowed to have their families and belongings with them. They were supported by the king to the tune of between one penny to 10s a day. Prisoners of state were at the mercy of the king and could either face the death penalty or be freed once he had calmed down.

PUNISHMENTS

In between fines and the death penalty, were a range of punishments including branding, whipping and the pillory or the stocks. And there is evidence that occasionally the defendant could even be offered a limited choice to reflect his or her individual circumstances. Sentences were almost always in public, since the humiliation itself was a large part of the punishment, and usually drew a large crowd.

Since there was no appeal procedure available to the majority of prisoners, the period between sentencing and punishment was generally short unless, as in the case of pillorying, the sentence was to be carried out on several occasions over a period of time. Then the accused would be brought back to Newgate after each pillorying to await the next. The death penalty was carried out on specified days throughout the year so after sentencing the condemned would have to wait for the next one to roll around.

Although it might not seem like it, the authorities, as today, were treading a fine line between the need for effective crime deterrents and the desire not to appear overly harsh. They had the power to commute sentences and often did, particularly in cases that carried the death penalty, but it was felt the crime was too minor to warrant such a drastic punishment. It had the double benefit of making the authorities look magnanimous while hopefully making the prisoner so grateful they would not re-offend.

All punishments applied regardless of sex, with some refinements to allow for women's decency. In theory they could also apply to children though those younger than twelve would be spared. In 1376, Robert Multon, a cook, was fined and sentenced to eight days in Newgate because his young apprentice had mixed feathers into a parsley stuffing but 'was too young to be punished'.

Fines

Fines and confiscation of property were at the lowest end of the punishment scale in medieval England. Since most crime was property-related, they were seen as by far the most popular and appropriate penalties. Fines were imposed for assaults and slander, and could also be paid to reduce or avoid a prison sentence, which made them a handy source of revenue as well as a means of reducing overcrowding.

Imprisonment

Imprisonment was seen as a sentence in itself from the thirteenth century onwards, though generally it was in conjunction with a fine, the pillory or flogging. Examples included: brewers selling short measures and beer that was unfit for consumption; candle-makers using impure cotton and tallow; and breakers of the City ordinances.

Imprisonment could also be commuted or bail could be granted which would help regulate the prison population and prevent overcrowding, as well as offering the option of a more lenient sentence should the case require it. On the whole, possibly because they added to over-crowding, very long sentences weren't popular.

There is evidence that sentencing was adapted to respond to crime waves or to be in line with prevailing attitudes to property. In 1327 John atte Gate, a thief, was imprisoned for eight days for the theft of 10d, while thirty-six years later in 1363, Alexander de Nedelere was imprisoned for forty days for the same offence.

The most common term was a year and a day, though days, weeks, years and, rarely, life could also be imposed. Records of only eight cases of life imprisonment survive from the fourteenth century, which is not surprising since a criminal could be hanged for stealing goods worth more than 12½d. Of these, six refused to enter a plea. One, William Bowyer, was convicted of hiring an assassin to kill Ralph Kesteven, the parson of St Botolph without Aldgate. Another, Richard Karlel, threatened and assaulted jurors at the King's Bench and it seems also refused to enter a plea, possibly in an attempt to avoid the confiscation of his property which would have been automatic if the verdict had gone against him. He was sentenced to life in the Tower.

The Pillory

The pillory and the stocks were ancient punishments dating back to Anglo-Saxon times aimed more at causing shame and humiliation than physical pain. There were pillories all over London, always in market places or busy shopping streets and the one most favoured by the authorities was on Cornhill. When settlements were small and everyone knew each other they must have been highly effective, since they exposed the incumbent to the maximum amount of ridicule from his friends, neighbours and business associates. For this reason, the pillory was the most popular punishment for cheats, perjurers, counterfeiters, scolds, sodomites, blasphemers, fighters and prostitutes. Examples of deceit include: selling underweight bread, dyeing old furs to look like new and hiding old fruit under fresh. The stocks confined a sitting prisoner by the ankles with his legs held out in front of him and compared to the pillory it was relatively comfortable. They weren't much used by the time Newgate was founded as the courts preferred the pillory.

At its most basic, this was a moveable wooden post topped by a lockable hinged framework with holes for the head and hands, but some were permanent structures raised up high so everyone had a good view and an illustration from the seventeenth century shows a revolving pillory, which the prisoner had to rotate so as to show his face to the whole crowd.

Men in the pillory were stripped to the waist and since this was considered an affront to a woman's decency there was a specially adapted pillory for women known as a thew. It was an upright post to which the woman was fixed by a collar, leaving her arms and hands free.

Whereas time in the stocks could be anything from one hour to three days, time in the pillory was measured in hours, one hour being the most common. Once locked inside there was no escape from the rotten cabbages, filth, fish guts, faeces and dead cats (a favourite) that would be hurled by the onlookers. Sometimes the spectators would collect their own missiles but they would also be available to buy from specially-loaded carts nearby. Sometimes though, if the prisoner was popular, or the crowd felt an injustice had been done, it gathered to offer friendly encouragement and support and a collection would be taken to help the family.

Generally, a prisoner sentenced to the pillory would have to endure more than one session at a time, place and duration specified by the court, so the sentence would also include a spell in gaol to prevent them absconding between sessions. A written description of the offence would be nailed to the pillory and the prisoner would usually be made to wear some visual evidence of it around their necks - examples include underweight coal, rotten meat, whetstones or even, in a case of imitating a physician, a urinal. If it was not suitable to be sent as charity to a prison, the offending coal, meat or fish might also be burned alongside the pillory.

Richard le Forester probably holds the record for the longest time in the pillory and given the strain the punishment inflicts on the back and legs, it must have been terrible. In 1320, le Forrester had tried to get Richard de Bentone to buy a garland for one mark that de Bentone knew was only worth 1d to 2d. Given that other thieves were sentenced to half an hour for similar crimes, the severity of his punishment suggests that this was not le Forester's first attempt at deception. He was sentenced to stand in the pillory from tierce to vespers, that is 9am to 4pm. After that he was banished from the City for a year and a day.

Sentences weren't consistent which indicates that judges applied their discretion, for example they were generally more lenient over the theft of food than the stealing of property, since people who steal food are generally desperate. In 1364, John de Hakford was convicted of perjury and sentenced to be pilloried four times over a year and a day. Each session was in a different part of the City and was to last for three hours. It was further decreed that he should appear 'without a hood or girdle, barefoot and unshod with a whetstone hung by a chain from his neck and lying on his breast, it being marked with the words "a false liar", and there shall be a pair of trumpets trumpeting before him on his way to the pillory.' The severity of this sentence may be because his crime threatened the Lord Mayor and Court of Aldermen.

In 1385, Elizabeth Moring was banished from the City for being a harlot and procuress. Before she was sent away she was made to stand in the thew for an hour, presumably so everyone could get a good look and recognise her if she ever tried to come back. The penalty for returning was a further spell in the thew and three years imprisonment. Since banishment was rare the severity of the sentence suggests that she was a repeat offender and that the authorities had lost patience.

The pillory and thew were severe punishments since, in addition to the physical strain, the victim was unable to escape the barrage of missiles flying towards him or her. These brought the very real risk of being knocked unconscious and dying of strangulation or a broken neck.

In 1413 John Askwythe was sentenced to the pillory for helping an adulterous chaplain escape. However due to his old age and frailty his sentence was commuted to a year and a day in Newgate. It is interesting that the court felt Askwythe would be better able to withstand a long spell in Newgate than a short period of public ridicule in the pillory.

Although members of the crowd were permitted to throw rotten vegetables, fish and other stinking rubbish at the pilloried prisoner, if he was injured they could find themselves facing a fine, imprisonment or death themselves. Death most likely would have been from a skull fracture or strangulation after being knocked unconscious with the neck trapped in the pillory. There are no records of death in the pillory in the late medieval period.

Branding

At the beginning of the Middle Ages mutilation: branding, slitting of noses, cutting off hands and ears, blinding, amputations had been a popular punishment but most forms fell into decline until only branding remained. Criminals were branded with hot irons on the hand with the initials V for vagabond, T for thief, F for brawler, M for manslaughter and S for a serf without a master. There was a short time between 1699 and 1707 when criminals were branded on the cheek but this was stopped because it made them unemployable. Criminals were branded at the end of the sessions in front of a crowd and it is alleged that petty thieves, and those who could afford it, paid to have the iron applied after it had cooled down. Branding was particularly shaming as it was a constant, public and indelible evidence of offending.

The last Newgate prisoner sentenced to branding appeared at the Old Bailey sessions house in 1789, but the punishment was not abolished by law until the 1829, after which it only applied to naval deserters who were tattooed with the letter D instead of being branded. Branding was abolished in 1779 as a punishment for those pleading benefit of the clergy.

Whipping

Whipping wasn't considered a particularly severe punishment and was meted out to beggars, vagabonds, vagrants and for misdemeanours not already covered by any other sentence. It applied to men and women equally and the lucky ones would be tied to a whipping post, stripped to the waist, and beaten across the bare back and shoulders. The less fortunate would be tied by the hands to the back of a cart, which would then be drawn through the streets, while the whipping was carried out.

Death penalty

The death penalty covered a range of punishments including straightforward hanging; hanging, drawing and quartering; burning; and beheading. While the Tower was the appointed site for the beheading by sword of nobles and royalty, Newgate was almost from the outset the hanging prison for London, Southwark and Middlesex. In time, prisoners were brought here from all over the country to stand trial and to be held until they were taken to the gallows or for burning at Smithfield. The condemned would be carried in a cart to the place of execution, usually Tyburn, through crowds lining the road. Sometimes the crowds were hostile, jeered and threw missiles, other times they were sympathetic and offered kisses and alcohol. The first recorded execution at Tyburn was of William Fitz Osbert, a former crusader and popular champion of the poor who led an uprising in the spring of 1196. He was dragged naked behind a horse to the gallows.

Public executioner was a formal appointment and the holder might even be a reprieved felon himself. He did not confine himself to hangings, since floggings, brandings, beheadings with an axe, burnings and hanging, drawing and quarterings were also in his job description. The executioner was in charge of the hanging: he chose the length of the rope, the position of the knot and how long the condemned would hang. It was a skilled job and care was taken to appoint men who could despatch the condemned as quickly and efficiently as possible. In the nineteenth century, a new system of hanging was developed to guarantee an instant broken neck but until then death was long, slow strangulation and could take around twenty minutes.

The more 'humane' hangmen swung on the legs of the condemned to hasten their deaths, or allowed the condemned person's family members to do the same.

Others climbed onto their shoulders or beat on their chests to cause a heart attack. If the rope broke, then the whole ghastly process would start all over again.

The death penalty was not nearly as widely used as might be supposed and the courts and juries found ways round it where they could. Around sixty percent of those condemned were reprieved.

Burning was the death penalty for heretics, martyrs and for women convicted of petty treason. Though its use reached a peak in the sixteenth century, there is evidence from the Middle Ages of people being burnt for their religious beliefs. In 1410, John Badby was condemned by the Archbishop of Canterbury as a heretic and sent to Newgate before being burnt 'as an example to other Christians'.

The reason for burning women was ascribed by the historian and chronicler Blackstone to 'the decency due to their sex [which] forbids the exposing and publicly mangling of their bodies, the sentence is to be drawn to the gallows and there burnt alive'. In practice though, the ever-compassionate executioner was on hand to strangle the woman before she was set on fire. Burning was abolished in 1790.

Beheading was reserved for nobles and royalty who would be decapitated with a sword to show their status. If a commoner was beheaded it would be with an axe to befit theirs. If the weapon was sharp and the headsman skilled, it could be a quick and painless death, but there are incidences of botched beheadings where it took several blows,

Hanging, drawing and quartering was a particularly gruesome and crowd-pleasing method of execution for male traitors during which the condemned man would be hanged, then cut down while still alive, castrated and disembowelled. Then his entrails would be burned before his eyes and he would be chopped into quarters. This was the fate that befell the popular rebel William Wallace in 1305 during the Wars of Scottish Independence. He was captured in Scotland and handed over to Edward I. After his death his preserved head was mounted on London Bridge where it stayed for many years.

Many hangmen either did not go through this whole ritual or at least they had the grace to wait until their prisoner was dead first. The last case was in 1820 and it was formally abolished in 1870.

ESCAPE CLAUSES AND OTHER ANOMALIES

Bail is an ancient means of mitigating punishment to the mutual benefit of the courts and the accused. It was a handy way of ensuring disturbers of the peace wouldn't reoffend, since they stood to lose not only their bail money but also their liberty. Debtors also qualified for bail since presumably they stood more chance of earning the money to settle their debts if they were free. As with today, bail could sometimes be refused

A pardon, a stay of judgement or execution, was a way of mitigating the severity of the death penalty. It could be granted to the insane, pregnant women who would 'plead the belly', children under the age of 12, anyone who could prove they killed in self-defence and anyone willing to serve in the army or navy instead. Pardons were granted by the king who was supposed to refuse them if they caused hurt or damage to others. Often they were issued at the last minute sometimes arriving too late, and dressed up as acts of Christian forgiveness.

A clergyman, or a nun, up for trial in a civil court could plead their vocation and ask to be tried in an ecclesiastical court in an exemption known as benefit of the clergy. Since the punishments in these courts were more lenient than in the civil courts, it wasn't long before regular criminals cottoned on. Benefit could commute a sentence from hanging to branding or whipping and up to a year in gaol or, later, transportation.

To prove himself eligible to plead benefit of the clergy, a prisoner had to be able to read the first verse of Psalm 51: 'Have mercy on me O God, according to Thy loving kindness' out loud. In the days when only the clergy could read this worked well, but a few rogues, such as William Hegge in 1406, took the precaution of learning the verse in case they were caught and eventually it applied to anyone who was literate, whether a member of the clergy or not. In 1598, the playwright Ben Jonson used it to get off after killing a man in a duel. Because the church courts offered more lenient punishments, the secular courts turned a blind eye to its misuse so that people would not be hanged for relatively minor misdemeanours. It became known as the 'neck verse' since that's what it saved.

Handily for the repeat offender operating before the end of the fifteenth century, there was no limit to the number of times benefit could be used. It was reformed under the Tudors so that by the end of the sixteenth century, criminals were only allowed to plead benefit once (unless they really were clergymen or nuns). After the first time they were branded on the thumb. 'Unclergyable' offences were defined and included murder, rape, poisoning, petty treason, burglary, theft from churches and pickpocketing. In 1623 women (that is, not nuns) guilty of stealing goods worth less than 10s were also allowed to plead benefit and in 1691 they were granted the same rights under it as the men. It was abolished in 1827.

Even though the penalty for escaping gaol was instant death by beheading, Newgate saw its fair share of escapes in the Middle Ages and beyond, probably because men facing the death penalty have little left to lose. In 1296, the law was changed so that if a prisoner escaped, the punishment was on the keeper who received a fine or imprisonment. This was further amended in 1504, when a sliding scale of fines calculated on the seriousness of the offence was introduced under the Statute of Escapes. Theses ranged from 100 shillings for accused felons to over 100 marks if the charge was high treason. The keeper was also responsible for recapturing the escapee at his own expense, though he could be pardoned if he succeeded.

The best escape route was over the rooftops, since if successful, it left no trace and it could be a while before the escape was discovered. It also helped get the prisoner far away from the gaol and into another part of the City with super-quick efficiency. Other methods included rushing the gates and making holes in the walls, while the other inmates sang psalms to cover the noise, but the worst was trying to get out along the sewers. Sometimes the escapees were assisted. In 1325, Johanna de Grendon was sent to Newgate for supplying the breakout tools for an escape; it was an expensive crime since it cost her her life.

When the escapes were successful, a posse would be assembled to hunt the escapees down for a reward, much like the American system seen in westerns. If the escapees managed to avoid recapture they could claim sanctuary in a church and negotiate exile abroad in exchange for their lives. This wasn't always the case though, as there were occasions when the sanctity of the church was violated and the prisoners dragged back to gaol. As an indication, in the absence of figures for Newgate, ninety-nine prisoners of the Marshalsea who escaped in 1470 remained free. Of course, if a person were innocent and managed to escape, they could set about proving their innocence. Debtors who remained free were laughing as the warden and the sheriff became liable for their debts.

NEWGATE'S INMATES

Although many of the prisoners have been forgotten forever by history, a good number of records have survived to show the variety of crimes and the statuses of those who committed them. Here are the tales of a baker, a knight and a bureaucrat.

William atte Sele

William atte Sele was a baker in the early fourteenth century from Bridge Ward, a small ward near the north end of London Bridge. In the 1320s, the price and weight of bread was strictly regulated, and he was caught using 'moulding-boards' which allowed him to bake underweight bread, which he then sold for the regulated price. Sele was not working alone. He was charged alongside eleven others, nine men and two women (who tried to put the blame on their husbands), all of whom were found guilty and sent to Newgate. The men were also sentenced to stand in the pillory for two days, eight of them with dough necklaces as the evidence had been found in their houses. The women suffered a similar fate in the thew. In some ways that William atte Sele was lucky; by the end of the century, the punishment for deceitful bakers was to be dragged through the streets on a hurdle - a panel of fencing made of intertwining branches.

Curiously, sixty years later, another William atte Sele of the same ward was found guilty of bribing officials to turn a blind eye to the same crime. He was fined 20s and bound over to make bread of the correct weight, under a penalty of

£40. This was not his first offence as he had already been condemned twice to be dragged through the streets on a hurdle with his loaf around his neck. Was this the same man or his son, perhaps?

Sir Thomas Mallory

Sir Thomas Malory was the author of *Le Morte d'Arthur* a reworking of the tales of the legendary King Arthur and his Knights of the Round Table. There were a number of Thomas Malorys at the time who could have been the writer but the one most agreed upon was from Newbold Revel in Warwickshire and lived between 1415-1418 and 1471.

Until his thirties, this Thomas Malory did well holding positions as a sheriff, a justice of the peace and an MP. By October 1441, he had been knighted and taken up arms as a professional soldier serving under the Duke of Warwick. After that things started to go wrong; in 1443, the year he was elected MP, he was charged with violent robbery, but the case didn't go to court. All went quiet for almost ten years, then in 1451 Malory seems to have got into a whole heap of trouble and the authorities threw the book at him. Charges included rape, extortion, theft, damage to property and the attempted murder of the Duke of Buckingham, and he was sent to gaol to await trial. Over the next eight years he was held in the Tower, the King's Bench, Ludgate and Newgate while he tried to persuade the authorities, against their better judgment, to swear a jury of Warwickshire men who were likely to look kindly on a fellow countryman in the dock. He escaped twice and was, surprising as it may seem, let out on bail. Each time he came back it was with further charges against him.

As a gentleman with supporters and family he would have had a reasonably comfortable time on the masters side of the gaol and would have been well-supplied with food, his own clothes and any home comforts he desired. His fellow prisoners would have also been men of standing and education so he would have had access to books and erudite conversation. It was in Newgate that he wrote part of *Le Morte d'Arthur* with paper quill and ink that visitors could have supplied or he might have sent someone out to buy from a local bookseller. The colophon to *Book VIII* holds the plea:

> 'All jentylmen and jentylwomen that redeth this book of Arthur and his knyghtes from the begynnyng to the endynge, praye for me whyle I am on lyve that God send me good delyveraunce. And when I am deed, I praye you all praye for my soule.'

It must have worked because in 1461 Edward IV pardoned him, not that Malory was grateful. By 1468 he was up to his ears in a plot to overthrow Edward, which landed him back in gaol. He was finally released in 1470 and died on 14 March 1471. He is buried in Christ Church Greyfriars, not so far from Newgate Gaol.

Thomas Usk

Thomas Usk's date of birth is unknown, but he was probably in his mid-thirties when he died in 1388. He was clerk of the closet to John of Northampton, who was a reformist Lord Mayor of London until he was ousted by a rival faction in 1383. In the ensuing scramble for power, Usk was gaoled but, with no wish to be 'a stinking martyr', he grassed on Northampton, who was then imprisoned while Usk was released.

For a while all was well, he rose through the ranks and was promoted to under-sheriff of Middlesex in 1386. However, this was the turbulent reign of Richard II and when the king fell so did Usk. The enemies he had made giving evidence against Northampton were now out to get him, he was seized again and, in the Merciless Parliament of February 1388, convicted of treason and sentenced 'to be drawn, hung and beheaded, and that his head should be set up over Newgate'. He was executed on 4 March 1388 and it took thirty blows of the axe to decapitate him after he had been hanged.

While in Newgate for the second time, Usk wrote the long and self-justifying *Testament Of Love*, an allegorical prose work written to appeal for aid and which, ironically, was for centuries attributed to his far more accomplished contemporary Chaucer, with whom he was probably acquainted

Chapter 3
Newgate under the Tudors and Stewarts
1500 - 1699

Over the sixteenth and seventeenth centuries, conditions at Newgate improved very little, though it seems the Court of Aldermen kept a close eye on things and did their best, if not to bring about 'the reformation of abuses by the keeper of Newgate against the prisoners', at least to stop conditions getting very much worse. Their ordinances covering repairs, escapes, mismanagement and charity appear, in the best traditions of council bureaucracy, to have been well-intentioned but ineffectual and the complaints of mistreatment, abuse of power and overcharging, especially of meat and drink, continued. It is possible that the Council and sheriffs were appointing the wrong people to the position of keeper, it is also equally possible that the prisoners' complaints were exaggerated to bring the greatest amount of sympathy to bear on their plight. It was probably a mixture of both since the keepers were ruthless racketeers and the prisoners were among the most desperate and dangerous in the country - quick to riot and quicker to complain. With nothing to do all day except drink, smoke, gamble and have sex, they continued to be rowdy and difficult to control.

The gaol itself was still the one built from Dick Whittington's bequest in 1423, and it regularly held double its capacity of 150 until the end of the seventeenth century when it was badly damaged in the Great Fire of 1666 and repaired. Life inside must have been pretty grim. Not that the mayor and aldermen ever went inside, at least not regularly. Fear of disease, the stench and the prisoners kept them away and, anyway, by 1539 they had a swanky new sessions house next door so the prisoners came to them. It was built on Old Bailey with a small garden where the judges could take the air between cases, and avoid gaol fever, but not the smell. It seems the sessions house was open-air because in 1550 a shed was erected to keep the prisoners dry and in 1562 another was built for the jury. It was extended again in 1568 and thirty years later the bail-dock was enlarged so the jury also got benches to sit on.

In 1500, seven prison inspectors were appointed to inquire into and report on the conditions in Newgate and, in 1550, the keepers of the City gaols were again ordered to run their prisons lawfully, which implies they had not been doing so.

William Crowder, who was keeper around 1580, drew considerable fire from the prisoners who complained that he and his wife were 'the most horrible blasphemers and swearers', took bribes and levied extortionate fines. Crowder had friends in high places including the Lord Chancellor and when he refused to help the enquiry into the complaints, the case was dismissed. Crowder was pensioned off, but he wasn't the last keeper to have complaints made against him.

So while life on the masters side continued to be relatively luxurious, life on the common side was anything but, with prisoners sleeping on mouldy boards fixed into the walls and dependent still on charity for their bedding, candles, clothing and food. The only thing that was free were the lice which crunched beneath the feet and swarmed over the body. But even so, the common prisoners were better off than those in the damp underground chambers loaded with irons and kept in the dark.

In 1558 the authorities tried unsuccessfully to ban the practice of prisoners begging in the streets, which had been introduced in the previous century. Another attempt was made in 1674, but that too was unsuccessful.

In 1571, presumably to cope with demand, the gallows at Tyburn was rebuilt. The new structure was the famous Tyburn triple tree, also known as the 'three-legged stool' or the 'three-legged mare', it was a vast permanent triangular structure that allowed twenty-four people, eight on each beam, to be hanged at the same time as on 23 June 1649, when twenty-three men and one woman were dispatched from it.

In 1617 the prisoners rioted about the lack of food and the unfair rationing of what there was. A Proclamation For Reforming Of Abuses In The Gaol Of Newgate issued afterwards states,

'Whereas of late, notorious mutinies and outrages have been committed by the prisoners within the gaol of Newgate, which is conceived to grow through the negligence of the keepers in suffering their prisoners to become drunk and disordered, permitting them wine, tobacco, extensive strong drink, and resort to women of lewd behaviour. By reason of which liberty, dissolute and lewd persons who commit thefts and robberies, take a kind of comfort, and gather heart in the said gaol, and are... intent to commit felonies, upon the hope of lewd company and such lewd comforts as they find in said gaol.'

It was yet another attempt at curbing the tyranny of the keepers and the misbehaviour of the inmates. The keeper for his part was only permitted to charge the authorised fees and charging for easement of irons was stopped. He wasn't allowed to accept gifts from the prisoners, and the amount of beer and tobacco in the gaol was to be restricted. The proclamation was also very strict about the fraternisation of men and women who would only be allowed to meet at chapel services unless they were known to be closely related.

The prisoners for their part were expected to improve their behaviour. To help this, they were forbidden from playing gambling games such as cards and dice, which seems a bit harsh given there was nothing much else to do. And the punishment for rioting or insurrection was a spell in the dungeons loaded with irons. It must have all been very bewildering for poor old William Cooke a stationer who was sent to Newgate in the early 1600s for failing to get planning permission for a shed he was building in Holborn for his stock. Hardly a career criminal, he would hopefully have lodged on the masters side. The architect Inigo Jones wrote drily on the impact of the sentence noting 'He lies in prison and the shed grows'.

Despite the proclamation, conditions in the gaol did not improve. In 1626, Sir Nicholas Poyntz complained he was held in a room with virtually no light and that he had to sleep in a coffin, while another inmate said 'he'd lain in a dungeon for fourteen days without light or fire living on a halfpenny worth of bread a day'.

Forty years later in 1658, the revolutionary idea of prisoner employment was discussed but nothing came of it and it would be another hundred and fifty years before a programme of work was implemented.

Seventeenth century officialdom was no different from today's in its love of committees and in 1630 another one was a set up, this time to look into prisoners' complaints that they were not receiving the charity they were due. This time it was the steward Henry Woodhouse who was under investigation for embezzlement. The committee, possibly seeing they were onto a nice little earner themselves, took two years to examine the complaints but, when they finally ruled, it was in the prisoners' favour. Woodhouse was fired and it was decided that, thereafter, the aldermen should be responsible for the quarterly distribution of all the prisoners' charity of £55 8s 4d a year. As a result, in 1633 a new system of self-governance was introduced to the prison from Ludgate Gaol. At a monthly meeting, prisoners would discuss their grievances and elect a new steward and cellarmen from among their peers. The prisoner-steward would take over Woodhouse's lodgings, his wages of 12d a week and would be entitled to double rations. By getting rid of the steward and handing the day-to-day management of the prisons to the prisoners themselves, the authorities had removed a layer of officialdom and further absolved themselves of an area of responsibility. However, since the prisoner-stewards quickly became as corrupt as Woodhouse, the complaints did not stop. By the middle of the eighteenth century, the system had simplified to the point where the keeper appointed four 'partners' who then appointed the cellarmen and women. Visits were still unrestricted and security was poor. Visitors were allowed to bring in food, clothing, entertainment and home comforts to help the prisoners make the best of their time in Newgate. In 1649, this was taken to extremes when a group of prisoners' wives attended a funeral service for their husbands who were due to be hanged. They had come into the chapel with rapiers, daggers and swords hidden in their clothes and as the sermon finished they rushed forwards brandishing the weapons to arm their men. In the brawl that followed, fifteen prisoners escaped and several turnkeys were injured.

The following year, the prison staff were banned from helping themselves to the prisoners' bread.

A programme of repairs costing £384 was implemented in 1629. Newgate was now 200 years old and the keeper complained of 'the great ruins of the gaol'. It was usual in periods of rebuilding to free a number of prisoners to reduce overcrowding and minimise the risk of escape and twenty-four pardons were duly granted. But the extent of improvements that could be made with early seventeenth construction knowhow to a medieval building were limited and, before he was executed in 1662, Colonel John Turner called it a 'most fearful sad deplorable place', where prisoners 'lie like swine upon the ground, one upon another, howling and roaring - it was more terrible to me than death'. By now the prison had taken over Newgate's ancient city gate, which was four storeys or sixty feet high. The lodge, condemned hold, and a dungeon twenty feet by fourteen were on the south side of Newgate Street and stretched back as far as the Old Bailey sessions house. What it really needed was rebuilding.

RELIGIOUS PERSECUTION

If the conditions did not change, the prisoners did. Under the Tudor dynasty, England endured its worst period of religious persecution and, depending on the way the spiritual wind was blowing, Catholics or Protestants found themselves in Newgate, awaiting burning at Smithfield or hanging, drawing and quartering at Tyburn where in 1537 the leaders of the Pilgrimage of Grace met their ends at the orders of Henry VIII.

After witchcraft was defined by Henry VIII under an act of 1542 as a felony, the guilty were hanged instead of being burned but they still forfeited all their goods and chattels.

Between 1535 and 1681, around 300 Catholic martyrs were executed while the sixteenth-century martyrologist and clergyman John Foxe records that at least 300 Protestants were executed for their beliefs under Mary Tudor alone.

Right at the centre of this were two men, the Bishop of London Edward Bonner and the keeper of Newgate Alexander Andrew, known as Andrew Alexander, or just Alexander.

Edmund Bonner was well-known for his assiduous campaign against Protestants; his contemporary John Foxe, in his *Book of Martyrs* called him 'this Catholic hyena'. Bonner was made Bishop of London in 1539 by Henry VIII as a reward for his help in annulling his marriage to Catherine of Aragon and he was regarded as being dictatorial and overbearing, unscrupulous and coarse. He freely admitted he was no theologian.

Alongside Stephen Gardiner, the Bishop of Winchester, Bonner was imprisoned and deprived of his see under Edward VI for refusing to acknowledge royal supremacy in religious matters. After Mary came to the throne he was restored to the bishopric and after some initial reluctance threw himself into the business of persecuting Protestants. London resisted with riots and Bonner was attacked at least twice.

To combat this, Mary set up ecclesiastical tribunals with Bonner in charge. He became known as 'Bloody Bonner' for persecuting the Protestants and during his campaign it is estimated that 300 died. Among his victims were the bishops Ridley, Latimer and Cranmer and another notorious case involving a preacher called John Porter who had upset Bonner. The bishop had him imprisoned in Newgate where he was 'miserably fettered with a collar of iron about his neck, fastened to the wall and in a dungeon'. A bribe to the keeper got Porter's fetters removed and he was sent to a felons' ward where he began to preach again. He was taken back to the dungeons and 'oppressed with bolts and irons, where, within six or eight days, he was found dead'.

Bonner also had John Hooper, the Bishop of Gloucester burnt at the stake. When the same fate befell John Rough, a clergyman from the north of England who had sheltered the Bishop of Lincoln during a previous persecution of Protestants, Rough was horrified to find Lincoln sharing the bench with Bonner as one of his judges.

When Elizabeth I came to the throne, she refused to let Bonner kiss her hand and since he refused to accept her supremacy over the church, he was stripped of his bishopric again and sent to the Marshalsea where he languished for ten years before dying. During Elizabeth's reign, Newgate became a more popular place of incarceration than the Tower.

Alexander Andrew was appointed keeper of Newgate under Henry VIII where he was the scourge of Catholic prisoners; under Mary he pragmatically turned his attention to Protestants. His cruelty was considered excessive even by the standards of the time. John Foxe wrote that the brutality 'of gaoler, Alexander, keeper of Newgate exceeded all others. A cruel enemy of those that lay there for religion. The cruel wretch, to hasten poor lambs to the slaughter, would go to Bonner, Story, Cholmley and others crying "Rid my prison! Rid my prison! I am too much pestered with these heretics".' John Story and Sir Roger Cholmley were lawyers who were actively and notoriously involved in the persecution of heretics alongside Bonner.

Edward Underhill, a prisoner in Newgate in 1553 presumably on the masters side, wrote that Alexander and his wife used to take supper with the prisoners. Underhill was an accomplished musician and they enjoyed hearing him play. He told another musician Brysto:

'I will show you the nature and manner of them. They do both love music very well; wherefore you with your lute and I with you on my rebeck, will please them greatly. He liveth to be merry and drink wine, and she also. If you will bestow on them every dinner and supper, a quart of wine and some music, you shall be their white son and have any favour they show you.'

The pair kept the keeper and his wife entertained with wine and music for two weeks until Underhill became ill through the 'evylle savors and unquyettnes'. Despite his enemies petitioning the keeper to keep him in irons and show no mercy, the keeper's wife took him into their own quarters and cared for him there.

It is grotesque to think of Alexander and his wife enjoying a knees up, while in the dungeons beneath them eleven monks left, chained and standing, starved to death alongside those who could not afford to pay to have their fetters removed and go free.

But perhaps the pettiest, most spiteful act of cruelty was reserved for John Rogers. Rogers was the gentle pious vicar of St Sepulchre's, the church opposite Newgate. He held unorthodox religious views and was friendly with William Tyndale and Myles Coverdale, who had translated the Bible into English, and had even translated a part of it himself. When Bishop Bonner had him sent to Newgate for heresy in 1554, he devoted himself to the thieves and murderers among the common prisoners. He suggested that he and his fellow prisoners on the masters side should pay for all their own meals each day but eat only one, giving the rest of the food to the poor, but Alexander would have none of it.

Rogers was offered a pardon if he would recant his views but he refused. Eventually, he was told by Mrs Alexander to prepare himself for the fire, and he was burned at Smithfield in February, 1555. His last request was to have a few words with his wife, which Bonner denied. However, on the way to the execution site, his cart was met by his wife and eleven children – one a babe in arms - who were coming to say goodbye. When the driver stopped to allow them to talk, the City sheriff, Woodroffe, hit him on the head and made him go on. Foxe records that Rogers 'constantly and cheerfully took his death with wonderful patience, in the defence and quarrel of the gospel of Christ'.

He also notes with relish that afterwards Woodroffe was 'struck with a paralytic affliction' and died a few days later, and that 'Alexander, the severe keeper of Newgate, died miserably, swelling to a prodigious size and becoming so putrid that no one would come near him'.

All places of terror and horror worth their salt, need a ghost and Newgate was no exception. It took the shape of a black dog, which slunk over the walls and around the prison on the eve of an execution. It was supposedly the spirit of Richard Bayfield who had been sent to Newgate for trading in banned religious books. He admitted heresy and repented and then recanted, like, said Henry VIII's advisor Sir Thomas More, 'a dog returning to its own vomit'.

Hayfield was burned at the stake in 1531 having been refused the customary and more compassionate exit of strangulation at the stake. It took him half an hour to die and his screams must have been terrible. The legend took hold, though Luke Hutton, a highwayman, wrote eighty years later that it was merely the by-product of a guilty mind 'a black conscience, haunting none but black-conditioned people such as Newgate may challenge to be guests'.

Barthomolew Legate was an Essex cloth dealer at the end of the sixteenth century. In the 1590s he and his two brothers Walter and Thomas began preaching against the concept of the Holy Trinity. In 1611, Bartholomew and Thomas were imprisoned in Newgate, almost certainly on the masters side, where Thomas died. Bartholomew though wasn't forgotten, he continued to argue with James I, who needed to be seen to stand strong against heretics and the ecclesiastical establishment who were caught up in their own internal battles for control of the church, but without any real conclusion.

Determined not to let this drag on, Legate threatened to sue for wrongful imprisonment whereupon the church jumped into action. A full Consistory Court (an ecclesiastical court) was convened in February 1612, where Legate was found guilty of blasphemous heresy and handed over to the authorities for punishment. He was given the chance to retract his opinions, but he refused and was burned at the stake in Smithfield on 18 March, 1612. He was the last person to be martyred in this way in London and the second to last in the country. Edmund Wightman was the last, in Lichfield, just three weeks later.

While religious persecution was raging outside Newgate, or perhaps because of it, the Council of Aldermen had turned their attention to the spiritual welfare of Newgate's inmates. In 1544, this was temporarily entrusted to one of the chaplains at St Bartholomew's Hospital and in 1546, when Henry VIII gave Christchurch Greyfriars to the City of London, Newgate was placed under its administration and one of their clergy took on the part-time role of Visitor of Newgate, known more commonly as the ordinary.

The ordinary was paid £10 a year and his duties included two to three services a week, 'going with the condemned prisoners to the place of execution to exhort them to prepare themselves for God' and ministering to the destitute prisoners of Newgate. He was also an informer for the authorities and mediator in inter-felon disputes encouraging the return of stolen goods and negotiating with desperate men.

In 1595, the ordinary received a Communion table and a pulpit for his chapel along with Bible and Prayer Book, to put on them. It was to be nearly a hundred years before the congregation would be trusted with Bibles and Prayer Books of their own, but by then there were two services a day and chapel was compulsory.

These services would have been Anglican so, in 1611, the authorities were alarmed to discover that Catholic Mass was being celebrated in Newgate. It was stopped.

Like St Bartholomew's, St Sepulchre's, just across the road from the Newgate, also dates from the twelfth century and the three institutions had a long association. It was from here that the bell was rung at the start of a hanging day, thanks to wealthy merchant tailor Robert Dow, who, in 1605 left an annuity of twenty-six shillings and eight pence for the religious preparation of the condemned of Newgate. In addition to the ringing of the church bell, the bequest also paid for a handbell to be rung and three canticles to be intoned: one by the clerk on the night before the executions:

'All you that in the condemned hold do lie,
Prepare you for tomorrow you shall die,
Watch all, and pray, the hour is drawing near
That you before the Almighty must appear;
Examine well yourselves, in time repent,
That you may not to eternal flames be sent.
And when St Sepulchre's bell tomorrow tolls
The Lord above have mercy on your souls.'

The second verse was to be spoken as the cortège passed the church and exhorted the prisoners to beg for salvation, while the last was for the bystanders after it had passed and encouraged them to pray for the sinner and lead virtuous lives.

In 1620, the position of ordinary became full-time and the first incumbent was Henry Goodcole who received an extra £5 a year. By 1684 the incumbent had help with the Sunday service and in 1694 another minister was appointed to attend the condemned from conviction to execution.

Perhaps the most famous, and lucrative, part of the ordinary's role was to collect the biographies of the condemned prisoners. In the eighteenth century these became bestsellers, principally due to the efforts of Samuel Pepys' secretary Paul Lorrain, who was ordinary between 1698 and 1719. These flimsy, hastily printed pamphlets sold well on the days running up to an execution, especially if the subject was popular or notorious, and the clergymen made a fortune.

During the Commonwealth, Newgate was a repository for Oliver Cromwell's Cavalier enemies, though it continued to find space for debtors, women, felons, traitors and committers of misdemeanours.

John Lilburne, a Leveller known as Freeborn John, was sent to Newgate three times for offending once against the royalists, then twice against the Parliamentarians. In 1637, he was charged with distributing Puritan pamphlets against the policies of the Archbishop of Canterbury, William Laud. He was sentenced to the pillory but, when the crowd supported him and the punishment turned into a protest against Laud and the king, he was sent to Newgate.

He was released in 1640 on the orders of Cromwell and he fought on the Parliamentarian side in the Civil War at Edgehill and Marston Moor, but he fell out with Cromwell after the battle of Naseby in 1645 and was sent again to Newgate on a charge of high treason. By now Newgate was full of royalist officers so he cannot have had an easy time.

Lilburne was banished to the Netherlands, but he returned in 1653, was tried again and acquitted. Despite the popularity of the verdict, the authorities considered it was too dangerous to leave him at large so he was sent back to Newgate from where he was transferred to several other prisons before his eventual release.

After the Restoration, on 30 January 1661, the anniversary of the execution of Charles I, the bodies of Oliver Cromwell, his general Henry Ireton and John Bradshaw who had presided over the king's trial were hanged at Tyburn, after being dug up, as 'revenge' for beheading the king. Cromwell's head was later stuck on a twenty-foot spike and displayed outside Westminster Hall.

Chapter 4
The Great Fire
1666 - 1699

The Great Fire of London, which wiped out the devastating plague of the previous year, began early in the morning of Sunday 2 September, 1666, in a bakery on Pudding Lane at the north-east end of London Bridge. Due to a combination of strong westerly winds and dithering on the part of the Lord Mayor and the authorities, who did not respond fast enough to the danger, it destroyed eighty per cent of the medieval city before it burned itself out. Over 13,000 houses, eighty-seven parish churches, St Paul's Cathedral and most of the civic buildings were destroyed as it raged from London Bridge to Smithfield in the north and Fetter Lane in the west. Southwark was spared only because the Thames acted as a natural firebreak. The death toll is usually put at six, the recorded number, but it was almost certainly significantly higher since it would have been impossible to trace the poor, who rarely featured in any official records, and many bodies would have simply evaporated in the heat. Newgate gaol on the north-western edge of the fire was severely damaged and about eighty percent was unusable. The authorities had no choice but to rebuild it. In fact, the prisons were considered so important they were, before the churches even, the first City buildings to be rebuilt. And they were the only reconstruction projects to be granted a government subsidy.

The new gaol was finished in 1673. It was five storeys high. Fifteen condemned cells were added in 1726 and by the middle of the eighteenth century there were thirteen common wards and four masters wards. It was also more ornate than the old Whittington gaol with statues on its east and west sides representing Justice, Fortitude, Prudence, Peace, Security, Plenty and Liberty who had a cat at her feet in memory of Richard Whittington, which must have brought comfort to the inmates. And in fact one citizen complained at the time that, 'Newgate, considered as a prison, is a structure of more cost and beauty than was necessary; because the sumptuousness of the outside but aggravates the misery of the wretches within.'

But however sumptuous Newgate's external appearance, the inside was as bad as ever and a dungeon by the entrance gate known as 'Limbo' acted as a kind of reception centre for new arrivals and a holding cell for the condemned. An open sewer ran through its centre.

Along with a new prison came new ideas on the treatment of the prisoners.

In spite of Limbo, the aldermen were very keen that Newgate should be kept clean as there was by now an understanding that outbreaks of gaol fever were in some way related to the filthy conditions and noxious air everyone complained so much about. However, the inmates were adamant in their refusal to cooperate and so they were left in their own filth. In 1692, a surgeon was appointed from St Bartholomew's Hospital to attend to the sick. He didn't have to wait long to be called into action as there was an outbreak of gaol fever the following year.

Edward Ward wrote the following in the *London Spy* in 1696 after a visit to the nearby Poultry Compter,

> 'The ill-looking vermin, with long, rusty beards, swaddled up in rags, and their heads - some covered with thrum caps, and others thrust into the tops of old stockings. Some quitted their play they were before engaged in, and came hovering round us like so many cannibals, with devouring countenances, as if a man had been but a morsel with 'em, all crying out, "Garnish, garnish", as a rabble in an insurrection crying "Liberty, Liberty". We were forced to submit to the doctrine of non-resistance and comply with their demands, which extended to the sum of two shillings each.'

There is no reason to suppose Newgate inmates were any better off – on the common side at least – as in 1699, yet another committee, this time from the Society for the Promotion of Christian Knowledge, had a poke around the prisons of London and came up with some suggestions to clean up the vice and corruption, the laxity and understaffing, the swearing, drunkness, gambling and sexual abuse. The ideas were remarkably enlightened and way ahead of their time since they included individual cells for prisoners, the separation of the old lags from the new and replacing corrupt officials with respectable and honest members of society. They advocated banning the sale of wines and spirits and all charges, except for food and lodging, and suggested that women should no longer escape punishment altogether by pleading the belly. But the most revolutionary idea was that prisoners should be put to work, the men to hard labour, the women to the work they were trained for and that on completing their sentences they should be released into the care of the workhouse until they could find honest employment. It would be another hundred years before any of these ideas were given serious consideration. As if to prove their point, lack of prisoner supervision in the same year resulted in the suicide of a condemned man on the day he was due to hang, after his aunt smuggled the dose of opium, which killed him, into the prison with her. On searching his room after his death officials found a loaded pistol, which had also been smuggled in.

Opinion is divided as to whether Jack Ketch was the worst executioner ever or a clever sadist who enjoyed making his victims suffer. He was active in the 1660s and 1670s and his botched executions turned even the crowd, who didn't like to see the condemned suffer unnecessarily, against him.

In 21 July 1683, he executed William Lord Russell for his alleged involvement in the Rye House Plot, a supposed plan to assassinate Charles II and his heir and brother James, Duke of York, though Russell was later pardoned. There were complaints about Ketch's clumsy handling of the beheading since Russell suffered blow after blow though none was bad enough to kill him. The outrage was such that Ketch felt obliged to write and publish a letter of apology, though in it he blamed Russell for distracting him by not lying in the most suitable way.

Two years after the Rye House Plot was the Monmouth Rebellion. The Duke of York was now James II and a Catholic, which didn't sit easy with some of his Protestant subjects. The Protestant Duke of Monmouth, an illegitimate son of Charles II and therefore James' nephew, claimed the throne and set out to overthrow him in June 1685. Monmouth was defeated at the battle of Sedgemoor on 6 July and beheaded by Ketch on 15 July 1685. Knowing how Ketch had messed up other executions besides Russell's, Monmouth asked to be finished off with one swift blow. But after three Ketch gave up and said he couldn't do it. Sources disagree on how many blows were finally needed ranging from five, the official Tower of London view, to as many as seven with the prisoner rising up in between blows to beg for it soon to be over. It is also said that in the end Ketch had to draw his knife to complete the job.

These two executions made his name a byword for an executioner and there was another gruesome reminder of his tenure. In Newgate, there was a room in which the heads of rebels and traitors were preserved in pitch and tar before being displayed on spikes on key approaches to the City, most notably London Bridge, and later, since this practice carried on into the eighteenth century, at Temple Bar. It was also where corpses were prepared for the gibbet (a sort of hanging cage in which bodies were exhibited as a deterrent to the rest of the population) and was apparently where the condemned men were held immediately before they set out for Tyburn.

In 1662, the Quaker Thomas Ellwood was sent to Newgate for refusing an oath of allegiance to the restored king. On arrival he was put in this room along with the quartered bodies of three men, who had been executed three days before;

'I saw the heads when they were brought up to be boiled. The hangman fetched them in a dirty dust-basket out of some by-place; and, setting them down among the felons, he and they made sport with them. [He] took them by the hair, flouting, jeering and laughing at them; and then, giving them so ill names, boxed them on the ears and cheeks. Which done, the hangman put them into his kettle, and parboiled them with bay-salt and cumminseed; that to keep from putrefaction, and this to keep off the fowls from seizing on them.'

With typical black prison humour, this room became known as Jack Ketch's Kitchen.

NEWGATE'S INMATES

Three prisoner biographies from two centuries of religious dissention and persecution recall the lives of a highwayman, a liar and a Quaker.

Claude Duval

The idea of the gentleman highwayman owes its origins as much to real life as it does to romantic novels. While footpads and pickpockets belonged to an ancient order of thievery, the gentleman highwayman who enjoyed his heyday around the end of the seventeenth and into the earlier eighteenth centuries could just as easily have been a casualty of Cromwell's Commonwealth: a dispossessed cavalier who was on the wrong side after the fighting ended and who needed the income from robbery to survive. The man said to have given highwaymen their reputation for gallantry was Claude Duval, the son of a French miller who came to England as a footman at the time of the Restoration and worked for a nobleman, probably the Duke of Richmond. Why he left service and became highwayman is unknown but he appears to have been quite good at it, menacing the roads around Holloway between Highgate and Islington for ten years. The legend goes that he was gentlemanly and fashionable, never resorted to violence and the ladies loved him. On one occasion he stole fifty guineas from the Master of the Royal Buckhounds and on another he is said to have taken a reduced booty after the lady in the carriage danced with him. His career ended, predictably, in arrest and he was hanged at Tyburn aged 27. After his death his body was exhibited in the Tangier Tavern where it drew a large curious crowd. He is buried in St Paul's, Covent Garden.

Titus Oates

Titus Oates, born in 1649, was a priest sometimes known as Titus the Liar. He was not overly endowed with intellectual promise: his tutor at Cambridge called him 'a great dunce', but he knew which side his bread was buttered, joining the Puritan side during the Civil War and switching back to the Established Church at the Restoration.

In the early 1670s, while he was his father's curate in Hastings, he falsely accused a schoolmaster of sodomy and was jailed for perjury. In 1677, he joined the Royal Navy as a chaplain where he was accused of buggery, which was a capital offence. He pleaded benefit of the clergy and escaped death. After that he travelled through Europe where he visited the Jesuit community at St Omer and falsely claimed to be a Catholic Doctor of Divinity. After he was expelled from St Omer, he returned to London where he took up again with an old friend, Israel Tonge. Together they wrote a document accusing the Catholic Church of planning to assassinate Charles II. The king was warned of the plot and though not unduly alarmed, he nevertheless asked the Earl of Danby to look into it. Danby took the matter much more seriously and by August 1678, Oates had made forty-three allegations to the Privy Council against various Catholics including 541 Jesuits and a number of aristocrats. He also accused the queen's physician and the Duchess of York's secretary of planning to assassinate Charles. Given his reputation, it is amazing anyone believed him, or at least didn't look into the matter further. Instead, the list of accusations grew to eighty-one, Oates was given a squad of soldiers and began to round up Jesuits.

On 6 September, he swore an affidavit in front of an Anglican magistrate as to the veracity of his accusations, but when the magistrate was found dead in a ditch five days later, Oates alleged it was the work of the Papists and used it to whip up anti-Catholic fervour.

Two months later, he was accusing the royal physician, of conspiring to poison His Majesty. As a result, Charles interrogated Oates personally, catching him out in a number of lies and inaccuracies. Oates was arrested and put in prison. However, parliament forced his release a few days later and Oates was given an apartment in Whitehall and a pension of £1,200. He was a hero.

It took three years and the execution of fifteen men before the truth finally began to dawn. Oates was undeterred; he even went on to denounce the king and his Catholic brother the Duke of York, but he was arrested on a charge of sedition, fined £100,000 and thrown into Newgate.

Another four years went by and in 1685 on ascending the throne, the new king, James II, the former Duke of York, had Oates retried. He was sentenced to life imprisonment and to be whipped five days a year for the remainder of his life. He was pilloried outside Westminster Hall wearing a hat detailing his offence, perjury, and pelted with eggs. The second day he was pilloried in the City and on the third stripped, tied to a cart and whipped from Aldgate to Newgate - that is, from one side of the City to the other. The next day the whipping continued. The presiding judge in Oates's case was the famously severe Judge Jeffreys and he and his colleagues openly stated their regret that Oates could not hang for his crime. It has been speculated that they imposed what they considered to be the next best thing, a punishment they hoped would kill him. Jeffreys called Oates a 'shame to mankind'.

Oates did not die in gaol; on the accession of William and Mary, he was pardoned and given an income of £260. He died in obscurity in 1705.

William Penn

William Penn was born in October 1644 the son of Admiral Sir William Penn who had served under Cromwell in the Civil War. He grew up in Essex during Cromwell's Commonwealth where the diarist Samuel Pepys, who tried to seduce Penn's mother and sister, was a neighbour. Following the Restoration, the family realigned with the monarchy.

After school, Penn went up to Oxford where he was introduced to new ideas and thinking and found himself drawn away from the Anglican Church towards the non-conformist Quakers who were much harassed by the other groups. He became a reclusive scholar, associating only with other free thinkers and got into trouble for supporting the dean and theologian John Owen who had been fired. After this, his father sent him to Paris to be out of reach of radical ideas. The influence of the French court taught him better manners and to take care of his appearance but it didn't change his nonconformist thinking. Back in England in 1665, following a spell in Ireland, he discovered that the Quakers were as persecuted as ever; they were even blamed for causing the plague that was ravaging London that year and were arrested for trying to help the sick.

When, aged 22, Penn finally joined the Quakers, his appalled parents realising the effect this would have on their own social standing disinherited him. For the next ten years he lived in Quaker families and learned more about his new faith, becoming its first theologian, theorist and defender. He wrote its doctrine and defended it publicly, raising awareness of its cause.

This public defence did not go down well with Charles II, and in 1668 after writing a tract, *The Sandy Foundation Shaken*, Penn was imprisoned in the Tower of London until he publicly recanted. After eight months a negotiated settlement was reached and he was released.

But Penn continued to be a thorn in the Church's side and after more pamphlets and more arrests he was tried, in 1670, alongside William Mead, for preaching in the street, which he had done to test a new law on assembly. The judge was furious and he refused to let Penn have a copy of the charges brought against him, though this was Penn's right. Without waiting to hear a defence, he put pressure on the jury to come to a guilty verdict. Despite this, the jurors found in Penn's favour, whereupon the judge invited them to reconsider. When they refused he fined them a year's wages each and sent them and Penn to Newgate, Penn on a charge of contempt of court. The jury fought its case from gaol and eventually won the right of English juries to be free of judicial control. It was known as Bushel's Case and was also a victory for the use of the writ of *habeas corpus,* which frees those unlawfully detained.

Penn was freed, on payment of a fine, by his father who was dying and wished to be reconciled with his son. Penn senior also negotiated his son's protection with the king and the Duke of York.

By 1677 persecution of the Quakers had escalated to such an extent that a group of them, including Penn, bought a tract of land in America, and emigrated there. It prospered and eventually became the state of Pennsylvania, named in honour of Penn's father. However, conditions at home continued to be difficult for the Quakers and many of them ended up in Newgate and the Bridewell.

Penn married twice and had fifteen children, though six died in infancy. Penn himself died penniless in Berkshire in 1718, six years after a paralytic stroke left him incapacitated and is buried at the Quaker village in Buckinghamshire.

Chapter 5
Inside the Prison-republic
1700 - 1769

By the beginning of the eighteenth century, the renovated Newgate was, according to the political agitator and novelist Daniel Defoe, one of twenty-two prisons in London, and for most of the century, life inside carried on pretty much as it had done over the previous five hundred years.

With four masters wards and thirteen commons, the poor prisoners still vastly outnumbered the wealthy. The underground chambers still existed but there were also secure cells in the gatehouse such as the one from which Jack Sheppard escaped in 1724, which had a large ring fixed in the centre to which prisoners were bolted. There was enough slack in the chain to allow the prisoner to lie down on a bed or in a hammock

By now the prison walls were covered with centuries of graffiti: dates of sentencing and release; tallies of days inside; records of crimes committed; and pictures drawn with knives and candle smoke. Fees covered rent, bed, blanket and the blacksmith to fit the irons; and the keeper still took a cut of all the food, drink or money brought in, a percentage of the blacksmith's fee and a percentage of any money earned by the prisoners while begging or working. The exit fees continued to be applicable for everyone until the end of the century. Visitors were charged admission. Garnish continued to be charged throughout the century despite complaints and attempts to eradicate the practice, with those unable to pay, such as Elizabeth Bennet and the robber John Hall, obliged to surrender their clothes. Elizabeth Bennet was held in Newgate in 1742 for theft of a blanket. On entering the common ward, a room about 26 by 32 feet (8 metres by 10 metres) shared with around thirty other women, Bennet was asked by the cellarwoman, Elizabeth Newbury, for the shilling garnish. Since she had nothing with her but the clothes on her back, Bennet had no means to pay and she asked if Newbury would wait until she was in funds. Newbury refused, demanding that Bennet hand over her dress leaving her with just her petticoat and stays, which was the minimum acceptable clothing for a woman at the time. Bennet resisted whereupon Newbury swore at her and took the dress by force saying she would only return it on payment of the shilling. Bennet complained to the keeper and Newbury was sent for trial. Newbury explained:

'I was made a ward-woman by the partners, and when I got a shilling I always gave them ninepence out of it, and they told me if people had no money, I must make it, or else I must pay for it myself; and as for this gown, Bennet was starving with cold and hunger and pulled it off and I lent her sevenpence halfpenny upon it.'

The partners were prisoners appointed by the keeper to oversee the others. Some of the women backed Newbury, possibly because she was powerful and they didn't want to offend her, others kept their heads down and chose not to get involved. Newbury was found guilty of stealing the dress and branded on the thumb. While Bennet never saw her dress again, she was acquitted of the theft of the blanket.

The case so appalled the judge that the authorities tried to crack down on the practice. They did not succeed.

Apart from the English, who would have made up the bulk of Newgate's population, there were many other nationalities and races including Italian, German, Jewish, Irish, African and American. Most were thieves who had robbed their employers, others were charged with crack lay (housebreaking) or dub lay (entering with a key). Other crimes included murder, rape, arson, forgery, highway robbery, coining and bigamy.

At night, the male felons were now separated from those accused of misdemeanour, though they, and the women, mixed together during the day. By now debtors were held separately.

A fascination with prisons developed in the eighteenth century, and visiting Newgate became a form of entertainment, a sightseeing event for tourists, like seeing the lions in the Tower. The charge to get inside was high, but the queues ran round the block. On payment of another fee, visitors could also attend the funeral service on the Sunday prior to a hanging, or visit the condemned in their cells.

The inmates, both on the masters and common sides, now carried out much of the day-to-day running of the prison themselves. At the top of these prison-republics were still the keeper and his turnkeys, but under them were four prisoners appointed by the keeper and known as partners. The beauty of this system from the keeper's point of view, since he paid the wages, was that he didn't have to employ so many turnkeys. The partners managed the steward and the cellarmen, who were supposedly elected at monthly meetings, though in practice the keeper often side-stepped this and appointed his favourites. The steward and cellarmen were responsible for the cleanliness of the wards, slopping out, smoothing over problems, managing the charitable bequests and doling out the daily penny loaf ration.

The historian John Strype, who updated Stow's *Survey of London* in 1720, noted the wages for this work which was paid for out of the charity box and the 1s 3d entrance fee. According to him the steward's deputy received 6d a night and the 'scavenger' who got 5s 8d a month for, among other things, cleaning and fitting the other prisoners' irons. In the outside world, a scavenger was a cross between a dustman and a sewage collector, which gives an idea of his position within Newgate.

Pickpockets were at the bottom of this hierarchy. According to the robber John Hall, hanged in 1707, who wrote an account of his time in Newgate entitled *The Memoirs Of The Right Villainous John Hall,* 'a Pickpocket is no more Company for a Reputable Housebreaker than an Informer is for a Justice of the Peace'. Hall described Newgate as a university college and called a first time offender a BA, a more experienced thief had an MA or fellowship and a condemned man was 'Head of his Order'. To further back this up, the prison was known as Whittington's College and inmates addressed themselves as collegians. Although the capacity of the gaol was still officially 150, it continued to be overcrowded particularly before Old Bailey sessions. Not unsurprisingly, filthy and rudimentary sanitation conditions led to disease and more complaints.

Some of the rooms had special names. Limbo was the condemned cell-cum-reception area; Bilbows was for punishment; in addition to being the room where the heads and bodies of criminals were boiled in tar, Jack Ketch's kitchen was also the holding cell for those waiting to go off for execution. The Strong Room was a dungeon where Pitt, the keeper, sometimes stored corpses and Tangier was a common ward in the debtor's side called by John Hall, 'the nastiest place in the gaol'. The Buggering Hold was another room, which may have held sodomites. Or maybe anyone ending up there knew themselves to be buggered.

According to Hall, there were 'very neat and clean' wards on the common side, though they were for those who could pay garnish and his idea of neat and clean may be relative given all the other evidence. However, he may also have been comparing it with the ward in which those unable to find the 6s 8d garnish would find themselves. 'One would take [it] to be Old Nick's backside...' he wrote. 'The lice crawling under their feet make such a noise as walking on shells which are strewed over garden walks'. Rats kept the place 'clean', eating detritus and dung.

Clearly the women still weren't completely separated from the men as their behaviour made Hall blush: 'The licentiousness of the women on this side is so detestable that is it an unpardonable crime to describe their lewdness,' he spluttered.

Gaol fever was still a problem and episodes flared up again and again across the century. The worst recorded cases were in 1726 when eighty-three prisoners died of it and, as we have seen, in 1750, at what came to be known as the Black Assizes, when the disease was brought into the courtroom by prisoners attending their trials and killed sixty-four, including four judges and jurymen, witnesses, spectators and the Lord Mayor. But it wasn't until 1757 that a surgeon and an apothecary were given a formal contract to attend to the sick within the gaol. By 1758, when there was an outbreak of gaol fever, they were refusing to enter because the conditions were so appalling; with the prisoners lacking clothing, bedding and other comforts, they felt their efforts would be a waste of time, which shows how little things had changed in five hundred years.

The outbreak in 1750 led to discussions about the need for a new gaol. Predictably, nothing was done about it, though some attempts, heartily resisted by the prisoners, were made to clean up the gaol and a ventilation windmill was added to the roof in 1752. It did not improve things and the sickness spread to seven of the eleven carpenters who fitted it, killing them and members of their families.

Those too poor to bribe the turnkeys for medical treatment regarding other illnesses rotted with distemper, cholera, scurvy and itchy venereal ulcers.

The daily routine was much as it had ever been: prisoners on the masters side were woken at 7am by a bell when they emptied their chamberpots and had breakfast, there was nothing to do until mid-afternoon except drink and talk and gamble. The taprooms were usually run by the turnkeys' wives and with wine expensive at 2s a bottle, brandy cheaper at 4d a quarter bottle and beer at 1d a quart, the annual tap profit was around £400. A rival taproom, set up by a prisoner in 1730, was closed down by the sheriff and a still discovered in 1737 suffered the same fate.

In the middle of the afternoon (as was also the custom outside the gaol) the main meal was served. A proper dinner of roast meat for the masters side, bread and water for the commons, unless they could get food from outside. There was charitable provision for meat for the felons, women and debtors but this would be no more than once a week.

The day ended at 10pm with the prisoners locked back onto their wards by the turnkeys and cellarmen.

The prisoners had always been recalcitrant and difficult to manage, now, through the prisoner-republics they were using their initiative and collaborating. They became ever more expert at wheedling money, food, alms and drink from visitors and they pooled their expertise to help each other petition anyone they considered to be sympathetic to their cause, to better conduct their cases or to at least get favourable sentences. In 1789, a group of prisoners anxious to avoid transportation joined forces to refuse the Royal Pardon. In 1780, only one in eight had legal representation and a trial lasted on average nine minutes. There was no court of appeal.

In 1756 when the prisoners used their power to complain that the alcohol in the taprooms was 'hogwash', the sheriff made the keeper refund their money. And at the end of the century The Free and Easy Club's mission statement was 'to promote tumult and disorder'. It was banned in 1808. In addition to the frequent riots, which were extremely violent on both sides, the prisoners took out their rage and frustration on their fellow inmates. Other ways to pass the time included: cards; dice; skittles; billiards; fives; sex; football; whoring; selling stolen goods; smuggling; tormenting passers-by; and mock trials. The 'London Monster' Rhynwick Williams, who had been convicted of stabbing women in the buttocks with sharp instruments, made a living out making and selling artificial flowers in the 1790s.

Mock trials were taken very seriously and were part of the self-regulation of the prison-republic with the most senior prisoners taking the role of a court official or member of the jury. The oldest prisoner would act as judge with a wig of rags on his head. The accused would be a fellow inmate who had particularly angered the rest of the ward, for example the man who hogged the fire, or the one who cracked lice between his teeth and spat the bloodied skins against the wall.

The most common punishment was a kind of homemade pillory chair to which the prisoner would be tied, his head through the legs and arms outstretched. He'd have to stay there until his judges felt he'd learned his lesson, which could be as long as a week.

As part of a drive to keep Newgate clean, and reduce incidents of gaol fever the verminous poor prisoners of the common side were obliged to wash, though it was often difficult to compel them.

Some of the prisoners were merry as beggars, others suffered a dejection of spirits brought on by their situation, and also probably by starvation, and the late-eighteenth century reformer, John Howard, records boys as young as 12 and 14 were mixed in with hardened criminals. The poorest prisoners slept blanketless on the floor. Thefts of blankets and other valuables were rife, as were complaints. Other men slept huddled in twos and threes on boards fixed to the walls, or took it in turns. Others still slept in hammocks, if they could get one. Some of the more callous cellarmen would rob corpses of their clothes and would only return the body to its family on payment of a fee. When the taproom was closed, they bought beer from passers-by through the gates.

In 1750, measures were taken to clean the gaol up and alcohol was banned. The prisoners ignored the new regulations; they couldn't see why they, or the gaol, needed to be clean. And since visiting was unrestricted and security lax, they got visitors to smuggle alcohol in or simply begged it from passers-by through the grilles in the gatehouse.

Now the press yard was no longer used for its original purpose, it had been done up and held the nicest accommodation on the masters side. Fees for entry were whatever the keeper felt he could charge and could range from £20-500, though this broad spectrum probably relates to a spike after the Jacobite Rebellion of 1715 when Pitt, the keeper who'd recently bought the post, needed to recover his outlay of several thousand pounds. It also probably takes into account the length of stay. Pitt raised the rent for the press yard, charged visitors entry to his gaol and for playing games and drinking the fine wines he was now stocking. He made about £4,000 in four months. Prisoners were allowed to have their families with them and, in the 1720s, a Major John Bernadi married there. Cleaners cost

1s a week and a prostitute 1s a night. Inmates included army officers who hadn't supported the ascension of George I; a forger of bank notes; a mathematician and a classics scholar. The evening entertainment consisted of skittles, smoking, drinking and chatting and debating. Friendships were formed and it became a hotbed for radical literature.

Since visiting hours weren't restricted, these inmates could have their friends and family round for dinner, though anyone sitting up late into the night with a bottle or two of brandy had to pay a fine (in drink) to the turnkeys the next morning.

According to John Strype who updated Stow's *Survey of the Cities of London and Westminster* in 1720, the session house on Old Bailey was 'a fair and stately building, very commodious and with large galleries on both sides for spectators'. The courtroom was 'advanced by stone steps from the ground, with rails and bannisters is enclosed from the yard before it, and the bail-dock where the prisoners are kept until brought to trial is also enclosed'.

There was a 'stately dining room, sustained by ten pillars' removing the need for the sheriffs to entertain the justices in their own homes as had been the case before the sessions house was built, when the prisoners were either tried in the justices' own homes or in the courtroom within Newgate itself.

The proceedings of the Old Bailey were published eight times a year, that is after each session until 1834 and then ten to twelve times a year until 1913, when publication ceased. They had been going for 239 years and were the juicy equivalent of a court transcript, recording the emotion of the sessions, the anger, the lewdness and outrage of the accused, the terror of the man sentenced to hang. A French visitor Louis de Muralt called them: 'one of the most diverting things a man can read in London'.

Later the best cases were collected and bound together in two volumes called the Newgate Calendar. They were extremely popular and would be on the bookshelf in any early aspirational nineteenth century home alongside The Bible, Foxe's *Book Of Martyrs* and John Bunyan's *Pilgrim's Progress*.

By the eighteenth century, capital punishment was increasingly used as a deterrent to make an example of troublemakers, habitual criminals and rioters.

Between 1790 and 1902, 1,100 were hanged, though the deaths are weighted to the eighteenth century since by the mid-nineteenth century the death penalty, while still on the statute books, was often commuted.

Tyburn and the Tower were not the only places of execution. Sometimes, to further deter the population or to cause maximum humiliation to the condemned, they were taken back to the scene of their crime and hanged there. In 1733, Sarah Malcolm, a triple murderess, was hanged in Fleet Street and in December 1769 two weavers accused of 'cutting', that is maliciously breaking the threads on a loom, were hanged in Bethnal Green. Pirates, smugglers and sailors were hanged at the appropriately-named Execution Dock in Wapping.

Newgate – the old City gate and prison (c 1650) that was funded by Richard Whittington's bequest in 1423
Credit: The University of Toronto Wenceslaus Hollar Collection

The junction near today's Marble Arch where the gallows stood until 1783 after which it was moved to outside Newgate
Credit: a detail from John Rocque's map of London, Westminster and Southwark (1746)

The Manner of Execution at Tyburn
Source Tyburntree. wordpress.com

An engraving of Titus Oates in the Pillory
Credit: Robert Chambers' Book of Days

Through the case of William Penn, juries won the right to be independent of judges. Penn went on to found Pennsylvania
Credit: La Biblioteque Publique et Universitaire Neuchatel

Daniel Defoe in the style of Sir Godfrey Kneller
Credit: National Maritime Museum, Greenwich, London, Caird Collection

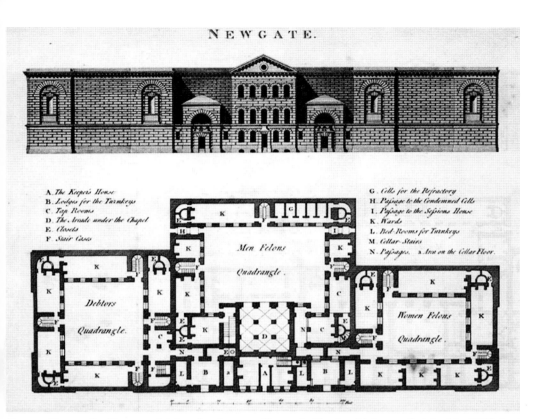

NEWGATE.

A. The Keeper's House
B. Lodges for the Turnkeys
C. Tap Rooms
D. The Arcade under the Chapel
E. Closets
F. Stair Cases

G. Cells for the Refractory
H. Passage to the Condemned Cells
I. Passage to the Sessions House
K. Wards
L. Bed-Rooms for Turnkeys
M. Cellar-Stairs
N. Passages.   a. Area on the Cellar Floor.

George Dance the Younger's plan for the new Newgate Gaol, which was finished in 1780, but was burned down within six months and rebuilt *Credit: The Crace Collection, The British Library*

Drawing of Smugglerius by William Linnell *Source: Wikicommons*

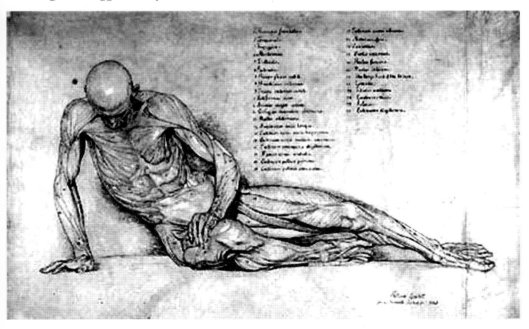

The mock invitation to the hanging of Jonathan Wild *Source: Wikicommons*

Painting of John Gay's The Beggar's Opera, Act V by William Hogarth, circa 1728
Source: Wikicommons

The Gordon Riots by Charles Green (1840-1898) *Source: www.mutualart/Artwork/THe-GORDON-RIOTS/OB3EC15174672097*

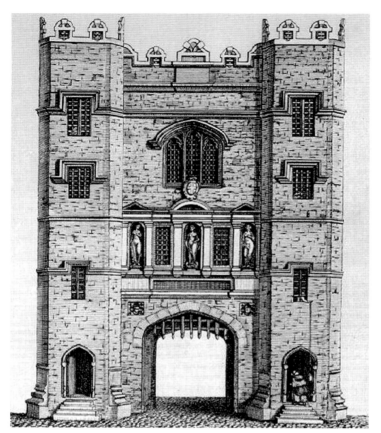

Newgate, the old city gate and prison from which Jack Sheppard escaped *Source: Wikicommons*

A sketch by Sir James Thornhill of the famous thief and prison breaker Jack Sheppard *Credit: The National Portrait Gallery*

The anti-Catholic Lord Gordon, who gave his name to the Gordon Riots which destroyed much of London in June 1780
Credit: Images Library, Yale University

Richard Akerman's house burning during the Gordon Riots
Source: englishhistoryauthors.blogspot.co.uk

A portrait of the prison reformer
John Howard by Mather Brown
*Credit: The National Portrait
Gallery*

Black-eyed Sue and Sweet Poll of
Plymouth, mourning their lovers who
are being transported to Botany Bay
by Rober Sayer (1725-94)
Credit: National Library of Australia

A west view of Newgate, circa 1810, by George Shepherd *Source: Wikicommons*

An execution outside Newgate in the early nineteeth century *Source: Wikicommons*

The Vere Street Coterie in the pillory. Note the dead cats and dogs at the top of the image. Circa 1810 *Source: Wikicommons*

Above: Mrs Fry Reading To Female
Prisoners at Newgate by Jerry
Barrett *Credit: The John Johnson
Collection of Printed Ephemera
www.johnjohnson.chadwyck.co.uk*

Left: Mrs Elizabeth Fry by Charles
Robert Leslie *Credit: The National
Portrait Gallery*

Below: The galleries and an
individual cell at Newgate 1896
Credit: From The Queen's London

William Calcraft who is estimated to have executed 450 people over his 45-year career *Credit: http://www. gertlushonline.co.uk/british-executioners. html*

The bell that was rung at Newgate on the eve of an execution. It was housed at St Sepulchre's *Source: Wikicommons*

There were eight hanging days a year; they could be on any day of the week, though Mondays became popular as it gave the chaplain a chance to hold the funeral service for the condemned on the Sunday before.

The condemned would be seated in the middle of the chapel often around a coffin from where, assisted by the chaplain, they would be encouraged to contemplate and repent their sins. During the eighteenth century, attendance at this and other services became a fashionable, if rather odd, form of entertainment for the well-to-do, so the condemned were further assisted by a congregation of nosy parkers and sightseers who had often paid for their seats. As if that were not enough, these sightseers were not above bribing the turnkeys to allow them into the condemned hold before an execution. Apparently, in 1724 the going rate to see the notorious jailbreaker Jack Sheppard was £200.

Everyone, it seems, apart from the condemned and their families, loved a hanging day. It was an excuse for a day off, especially among London's apprentices, and seen as a great celebration especially if the condemned were popular with the crowd or famous. There was no sense that capital punishment might be barbaric and inhumane, or an even an effective deterrent to other criminals. Pickpockets and prostitutes plied their trades among the crowds that gathered and the condemned's associates turned up to cheer their friend into the next life. The crowd was hugely partisan and not afraid to show its feelings, cheering its favourites and jeering and throwing missiles at those it reviled. Huge crowds, often as many as 30,000 strong, gathered at the gallows and there were hawkers, traders and souvenir sellers, pie sellers, gingerbread men and other fast food outlets. Gentlemen such as the writer James Boswell and high-born ladies rubbed shoulders with members of the criminal fraternity and the atmosphere was carnivalesque but with the added drama of ritualised death. And there was always the possibility of a last-minute reprieve. If it arrived once the hanging was in progress, the (un-)condemned person would simply be cut down and revived.

A typical day started early when the condemned, hands tied behind their backs, were loaded, five or six at a time, onto carts, sometimes seated on their own coffins. The ordinary and other prison officials travelled with them, which in the case of unpopular prisoners was sometimes all that stopped them being torn limb from limb as they passed along the route. The cortège would then rumble off to the sound of St Sepulchre's bell, which tolled from 6am-10am on the morning of an execution. The noise and size of the crowd that poured out onto the street or hung out of windows to line the route must have made their heads spin after so long cooped up in the condemned cell.

It is about two and a half miles, less than an hour's uninterrupted walk from Newgate along High Holborn, Chancery Lane and Oxford Street (Tyburn Road until the 1700s) to Tyburn, though on a hanging day this could take up to three because of the crowds and frequent stops for alcohol: almost no one went to the gallows sober. There were presents from the crowd of posies of flowers, kisses and more alcohol, if the condemned were popular; dead cats, bottles, rotten vegetables and faeces if they weren't. Armed guards on horseback rode alongside to prevent escapes and also to prevent the crowd mobbing the condemned for locks of their hair or pieces of cloth which were said to hold magical healing powers. The crowd didn't always approve of a hanging. If they thought there had been a miscarriage of justice, or the victim was very young or the crime didn't warrant such a harsh punishment they would make their feelings known to the sheriff and his men.

By unspoken tradition, highwaymen led the cortège to Newgate on hanging days. And the crowd loved them partly for their audacity and partly because they targeted the rich in their fancy carriages who, it was felt, could afford it. In 1732 John Waller was killed in the pillory for giving false evidence against them.

Some such as Dick Turpin and James MacLaine, had chosen the life over the more respectable ones originally planned for them. Turpin was to have been a butcher, MacLaine the son of a Scottish Presbyterian minister was educated to be a merchant. The politeness of highwaymen and their kindness to ladies weren't always the best qualities for the job, perhaps they were careless or perhaps the authorities got better at catching them but at the turn of the eighteenth century there were an inordinate number in Newgate. As much as £40 could be offered as a reward for their capture. Facemasks and scarves meant they weren't always easy to recognize, so an early sort of identity parade would be held in the area outside the gaol, where the highwaymen and their horses were walked around and anyone who had been robbed was invited to come along and pick their assailant out.

At Holborn or St Giles the cortège stopped and the condemned had 'one for the road' with the hangman to show there were no hard feelings. If they were 'on the wagon' they were at the sober end of drunk, if they 'fell off the wagon' then presumably they were drunk to the point of oblivion.

Many of the condemned wore their best clothes, if they had any. If a prisoner was wealthy or famous enough, they could customise their part in the procession. And some seeing it as their moment in the spotlight, their fifteen minutes of fame as it were, really went to town. The infamous Dick Turpin, wore a new suit and shoes and hired five mourners to walk behind his cart, while another highwayman (and dandy) Nathaniel Hawes refused to plead at his trial because he had had his clothes confiscated and he refused to be hanged in a dirty shirt. Mary Young, the leader of a gang of thieves, rode in her own mourning carriage.

A foreign visitor to London attending an execution in 1725 observed:

'When all the prisoners arrive at their destination they are made to mount on a very wide cart made expressly for the purpose, and a cord is passed around their necks and the end fastened to a gibbet, which is not very high. The chaplain who accompanied the condemned men is also in the cart; he makes them pray and sing a few verses of the Psalms. The relatives are permitted to mount the cart and take farewell. When the time is up - about a quarter of an hour - the chaplain and the relations get off the cart, the executioner covers the eyes and faces of the prisoners with caps, lashes the horses which draw the cart, which slips from under the condemned men's feet, and in this way they remain hanging together.'

Before the cart was pulled away, the condemned were allowed to make their final speech. Possibly in the hope that they would confess their sins - it was rarely fulfilled. Not that it mattered, since the speeches were rarely heard above the roaring crowd. Sometimes they merely said their thank yous, sometimes they had full speeches prepared in the hope that a reprieve might arrive before they reached the end.

Once the cart had been pulled away, the hangman or relatives of the prisoner would sometimes pull on the legs to break the condemneds' necks and speed up the process. 'Cutting down' marked the end.

The contemporary historian John Laurence described a hanging at Tyburn:

'Frightful scenes were witnessed at executions, the crowd standing awestruck as it watched the convulsions of the struggling culprit. Every contortion of the limbs was hailed with a cheer or a groan according to whether the sufferer was popular or not; appalling curses and execrations occasionally rent the air and rendered the last moments of the unfortunate criminal more odious; hawkers boldly sang the praises of their wares, while a fellow creature was being done to death. Rich and poor, thief and lord, gentle and simple attended "the hanging" and cracked jokes at the sufferers' expense.'

If, as happened occasionally, the hangman got it wrong and a man was cut down too soon, the 'corpse' would be taken away and resuscitated. The Newgate Calendar, an eighteenth and nineteenth century collection of Newgate's more lurid executions, carries the account of John Smith, a robber, who was hanged but survived to became known as Half-hanged Smith. The account of his ordeal said that:

'He was sensible of a very great pain, occasioned by the weight of his body, and felt his spirits in a strange commotion, violently pressing upward; that having forced their way into his head he, as it were, saw a great blaze, or glaring light, which seemed to go out at his eyes with a flash and then he lost all sense of pain.

'That after he was cut down and began to come to himself, the blood and spirits, forcing themselves into their former channels put him, by a sort of pricking or shooting to such intolerable pain that he could have wished hanged who had cut him down.'

John Smith was pardoned but the lure of crime proved too much. He was caught tried and acquitted on two more capital offences, once on a technicality and once because his prosecutor died before he was due to give evidence, making him one of the luckiest men ever to pass through Newgate's gates. After this he was never heard of again.

There was a great deal of superstition surrounding hanging. Often people would try and touch a dying man, or lift up a child to do so, in the belief that it would cure illnesses such as cancer. And the rope would be sold off by the inch as it was thought to bring luck.

After the hangings the crowd dispersed for more drinking; sometimes the bodies would be given up to the Royal College of Physicians for dissection but not if the friends and family got there first. Sometimes there would be a tussle for the corpse if it had been promised to both parties and, on occasion, if the crowd had other ideas the body was not taken for immediate burial. In one case where members of the crowd were very incensed that a man had been hanged, they took the corpse and laid it on his accuser's doorstep, then they ransacked her house, burned her furniture and threw stones at the soldiers trying to dowse the flames. Other times considerable efforts would be made to revive the corpse - very occasionally they were successful.

The eighteenth-century judge and politician Sir William Blackstone thought keepers 'a merciless race of men, and by being conversant with scenes of misery steeled against any tender sensation'. But there was one Richard Akerman who is probably the best known of all Newgate's keepers, and famously regarded as being the most humane. He held office as keeper for thirty-eight years until he died in November 1792. He was the deputy head keeper for at least twelve years before that. Records show that in 1742 he had three turnkeys under him named Wilcox, Nichols and Townsend. The first two were respected and considered fair, but the latter was 'despised by all that know him'.

Akerman was not regarded an extortioner by the standards of the day, and it is generally agreed that the size of his fortune, he left £20,000 in his will, at a time when a merchant would consider himself wealthy on £600 a year, was due more to his extraordinary length of service than excessive greed in dealing with his charges. He was married with a family and they lived on site.

Akerman was popular and much courted by society. In this he seems to have been unique among the keepers who, despite their wealth, were generally on the fringes: too rich to associate with the poor, too much in authority for the criminal fraternity and too rough for polite society. Akerman had a fan club which met at

The Globe Tavern on Fleet Street and, since he often went along, he cannot have been that averse to the adulation that surrounded him.

He was well-respected by his charges and did his best to help them out, supplementing the penny loaf diet of the most impoverished with a coarse meat soup paid for out of his own pocket. He understood the benefits of cleanliness and made efforts to ensure his reluctant charges kept their quarters clean. The reformer John Howard noted he 'generously contributed' to the upkeep of the poor prisoners.

Samuel Johnson praised him, writing, 'He who has long and constantly in view the worst of mankind and is yet eminent for the humanity of his disposition, must have had it originally in a great degree and continued to cultivate it daily.' Johnson's friend and biographer James Boswell and the statesman Edmund Burke were also enthusiastic supporters.

In the days long before there was any understanding of mental illness, Akerman reported to parliament on a depression among the prisoners, which was like a disease he felt, and which caused many of them to give up and die on entering gaol. These prisoners he observed were usually better behaved and less abandoned than the others. When prisoners were unruly he locked them up and put irons on their legs, observing 'They seem to dread solitary confinement'.

Some years into his tenure, a fire broke out in the gaol and a group of prisoners were at risk. In a great act of trust and at personal danger to himself, he rescued them and took them away from the fire to another part of the gaol.

From the end of the seventeenth century until the early nineteenth, the number of crimes in England punishable by death increased from around 50 in 1660 to 160 by 1750 to 288 by 1815. The death sentence could be applied for stealing goods worth as little as five shillings, stealing from a shipwreck or damaging Westminster Bridge. As the population and cities grew, the ruling classes became nervous that there would be an increase in crime, particularly against property. The Bloody Code, though it was never called this at the time, was intended as a deterrent to any would-be criminals. However, it was so draconian that juries often refused to convict and judges frequently colluded in reducing the value of goods stolen to bring the offence below capital levels, for example, 'Stole £5, value ten pence'. Sometimes they even let people off. In fact, despite its name, fewer people were hanged under the Bloody Code than before it. This was partly because that old get-out-gaol-free card benefit of the clergy provided an escape clause for both the prisoner and the judiciary.

In 1706, the reading test was abolished and benefit of the clergy became available to all first-time offenders of lesser felonies, though the minimum sentence after pleading it was six months to two years hard labour. In 1718, benefit commuted the death penalty to seven or fourteen years transportation to America or, after 1787, to Australia.

Although transportation was first permitted under an act of 1598, the first case was not recorded until 1615 when James I wrote in a letter that a 100 convicts had been sent to Virginia. Transportation wasn't a sentence in itself, but a condition of being pardoned and was introduced to plug the gap between the severity of the death penalty and leniency of the ecclesiastical courts. In a way, it was an extreme version of the medieval sentence of banishment. After serving their sentences the convicts were free to return home if they could afford it, or they were still alive. Coming home before the end of a sentence was a capital offence. The perceived benefits of transportation were threefold: it removed those who were a menace to society; acted as a deterrent; and it showed the king to be merciful in sparing life, which was never bad for his image.

While in theory transportation applied regardless of age or gender, in practice, the courts made efforts to spare women and children since they usually committed minor crimes and were not considered dangerous to the community. Transported women were generally sent to the Leeward Islands. Barbados and Jamaica expressly refused to take women, children and the sick.

Convicts were carefully selected for transportation. They needed to be fit and able to work and survive the voyage. On arrival, they would be sold as indentured servants, or as time went on, in the slave markets alongside the African victims of the slave trade.

Transportation wasn't universally popular in America, where people had gone to make a better life, and some of the states objected to having England's undesirables foisted on them. In 1670, both Virginia and Maryland refused to accept any more transports and the government was forced to respect this.

The Transportation Act 1717 legitimised and streamlined the practice making transportation a sentence in itself and it was not long before transportation became big business. In 1718, a merchant called Jonathan Forward won the contract to transport prisoners and was paid £3 per person (rising to £5 in 1727) to take the convicts across the Atlantic. Eventually, the merchants were doing well enough out of the enterprise that the £5 payment was considered unnecessary by the government and it was stopped.

In 1736, seven men awaiting transportation managed to escape from Newgate by breaking through the floor and dropping into the common sewer, followed by another later that year. But on another occasion, rescuers found the bodies of two men who'd suffocated during a previous attempt.

Transportation to the Americas ended with the outbreak of the American War of Independence and for a while there was a hiatus when no transportation took place and men and women were sentenced to hard labour instead. Australia had been discovered in 1770 so, when transportation resumed in 1787-8, convicts were sent there instead.

At the beginning of the eighteenth century people still policed their own communities, as had always been done, with a watch - often the watchman was an old man with a lantern, a staff and a rattle to summon help. With no police force to help them, victims of theft simply appealed for the return of their goods by advertising a reward in the newspaper and hoping they got lucky. Justice was dispensed by the sheriffs and judges, but as the population grew, crime increased and criminals became more sophisticated, the need for an effective and coordinated force arose.

Between 1690 and 1720 there was a dramatic rise in crime, which gives the lie to the thinking that the Bloody Code was some kind of deterrent. As a result, the maximum reward for securing a conviction for felony increased to £140, a vast sum when an artisan such as a carpenter would make between £20 and £30 per annum. Not surprisingly, it attracted a number of opportunists and self-styled thief-takers, who operated in much the same way as American bounty-hunters, and who were willing to go to the trouble and expense of tracking down felons and bringing them to trial. The most famous of these was Jonathan Wild and, though he was well-known at the time, his memory has endured because his manipulation of the legal system was the catalyst that triggered the founding of the police force.

Wild operated at the beginning of the eighteenth century, on both sides of the law, styling himself the Thief-taker General of Great Britain and bringing criminals to justice on one side while operating an organised crime syndicate on the other. It is estimated he had made a staggering £25,000 by the time of his death on 24 May 1725, aged 42 or 43.

To keep his large gang of thieves and false witnesses in check, and to impress the authorities with his investigative abilities, Wild would occasionally turn in a few of his confederates and claim the reward. Between 1716 and 1725, he gave evidence at thirty-six Old Bailey Trials and claimed his evidence had resulted in the conviction and execution of sixty-seven people including the petty thief and famous escaper Jack Sheppard in 1724.

The authorities, however, were getting wise to his actions but they could not prove anything until in February 1725, when Wild was arrested and put in Newgate. The official line was that he had helped one of his men escape from prison; however, eleven other crimes were also listed on the warrant. Wild continued to run his business from Newgate, an action that played straight into the hands of the authorities, who were keeping an eye on him. Meanwhile on the outside, his gang, emboldened by the length of time their boss was spending in gaol, and convinced that his time was up, started to come forward and give evidence against him. On 15 May, Wild was tried on two charges, one for the theft of 50yards (46m) of lace from Catherine Statham, a lace-seller, and the second for arranging the return of the goods without attempting to prosecute the thieves. Catherine herself had been to see Wild several times in an attempt to secure his help in getting the lace back, but he delayed helping her until finally she put an advert in the paper asking for the return of her goods and offering a reward. This forced Wild's hand, and worried that he would lose control of the situation and therefore the reward, Wild finally agreed to help. The whole story came out at his trial. The theft of the lace had been done at Wild's instigation - he had even been standing outside the shop while it took place. After the crime had been committed, the thieves and Wild all went back to Wild's house where he paid them. After the advert had been placed, he then arranged return of the goods and claimed the reward.

Wild was acquitted on the first charge of theft. But, despite pleading his work as a thief-taker in his defence and, suggesting that any evidence against him was given in the spirit of revenge, he was found guilty on the second charge and sentenced to death. He appealed for an acquittal on a technicality but it was refused. Wild was terrified; he couldn't eat or drink or go to church.

London's criminal underworld was not so unhappy. Gleefully, a mock invitation was issued to the execution of Jonathan Wild inviting all the 'thieves, whores, pick-pockets, family fellons, etc of Great Britain and Ireland' to see him hang.

On the morning of his execution, 24 May 1725, Wild tried to commit suicide by drinking laudanum but, because his stomach was empty from not eating he brought the dose back up. However, he'd taken enough for him to sink into a coma. He was the last man to be hanged that day, still stupefied by drugs and surrounded by a cheering crowd delighted to see him go. The hangman, Richard Arnet, had been a guest at his wedding.

Wild was buried in St Pancras Churchyard next to his third wife and is the basis of the character Peachum in John Gay's *The Beggar's Opera*, an allegory about Wild and Jack Sheppard's escapades that controversially drew parallels with Sir Robert Walpole's government of the time.

Wild's exploits as thief and thief-taker convinced the brothers Henry and John Fielding, who served successively as Bow Street magistrates, that a proper police force was needed. When Henry Fielding took office in 1748, he had 380 watchmen and eighty constables, only six of whom he considered trustworthy. These six were the start of the Bow Street Runners, which grew eventually, and with not a little help from Sir Robert Peel, into the Metropolitan Police Force we know today. They were paid from reward money.

After Henry's death in 1754, his blind brother John, known as 'the Blind Beak' expanded on his work setting up mounted and foot patrols and paying the men a salary though they were still allowed to keep the reward money. Although they had no official status, the runners carried batons bearing a gilt crown. Their success meant that some of London's criminals took their business elsewhere, so in 1772 John Fielding began circulating *The Weekly or ExtraOrdinary Pursuit*, containing lists of known or suspected criminals, to justices of the peace around the country. It was the first attempt at national criminal intelligence and eventually became the *Police Gazette*.

However, it was a while before the thief-takers were absorbed into the new system and one case threatened to undo the new reforms. In 1756 Stephen McDaniel and three of his band, were sentenced to be pilloried over two days at the end of Hatton Garden. They had been sentenced to death, but the crown had remitted this. McDaniel was no better than Wild and he was known to Henry Fielding but not used by him. He encouraged mentally vulnerable young men to commit robberies in a set-up where the victim, the accomplices and the receiver of the goods were all in on the scam. Their sole intention was securing a conviction and the generous reward. Three of their victims went to the gallows before they were discovered trying to prosecute two more. McDaniel and his fellow thief-taker John Berry were put in the pillory first. The crowd vented its anger and left McDaniel badly cut and Berry close to death. When it was the turn of the second two, James Salmon and James Eagan, the authorities must have known of the risk of death to the two men. Nevertheless, they were set in the pillory at Smithfield on market day.

'Eagan had one eye cut out soon, [and] after some Time, one particular Bone was flung at him in the Fore Part of his Head and Face, by which he had his other eye beat out, and with his struggling, through the Pain, got his Hands out of the Pillory; then being much stupefied with the Blow... his Legs gave Way under him, he soon appear'd as if he was dead, but was continued in the Pillory till the Time was expir'd, which was near half an hour.'

Two days later it was reported that Salmon was not expected to live.

People did not always get such harsh treatment in the pillory however. When the writer Daniel Defoe had been pilloried in 1703 at Cheapside and Fleet Street for seditious libel, the crowd cheered and his friends sold copies of his books. In 1765 John Williams, publisher of the *North Briton*, was put in Newgate on a charge of seditious libel after he printed an article by the political agitator John Wilkes, accusing the government led by Lord Bute of lying. Wilkes's status as an MP exempted him from prosecution so the government sued Williams instead. In the pillory, Williams was greeted by the 'repeated acclamations of upwards of 10,000 people', who collected 200 guineas for him and executed Lord Bute in effigy. Two years earlier, the crowd had also held a collection for two elderly men, one over seventy, who had been pilloried outside Westminster Hall.

After McDaniel's case there was a decline in the use of the pillory, possibly because of the new punishments being brought in.

Chapter 6
The New Newgate
1770 - 1799

Around 1768, in response to a campaign by the former Lord Mayor Sir Stephen Janssen, the City's newly-appointed, 27-year-old architect and surveyor George Dance the Younger was asked to come up with a design for a new gaol and sessions house. Janssen had been at the Black Assizes in 1750 when sixty-four people had died of gaol fever and he had been responsible for the ventilation windmill erected on the roof two years later.

Dance's design was radical and new; a blueprint for a building in the *architecture terrible* style that was so monstrously brutal in appearance that its very presence would act as a deterrent to wrongdoers. Or so the authorities hoped.

Unlike the leaky 250-year-old patched-up gatehouse gaol with its grilles and multiple opportunities for begging and escape, the new Newgate was a fortified citadel surrounded by high windowless stone walls. Handily, the building backed onto the Royal College of Physicians in Warwick Lane, which received the corpses of the condemned for dissection in its anatomy classes and it stretched down Old Bailey to where a new sessions house had been commissioned to include a single courtroom and a fancy dining room with a mosaic, a vault of fine wines and an expensive Turkish carpet. There was also a room for witnesses who had previously had to wait in the pub down the road to be called. The sessions house was completed in 1774.

Construction on the gaol started in 1770 when the Lord Mayor William Beckford laid the foundation stone. Newgate's new facade fronted onto Old Bailey, in the centre was a five-storey brick house where the keeper, Richard Akerman, lived with his family, secure studded doors on other side of this admitted visitors and prisoners to the gaol. There was a connecting door to the sessions house through which prisoners travelled to and from court. By 1775, two of the quads had been completed and the order was given to demolish the rest of the old gaol, the last part to be torn down was the gatehouse itself in 1777. Behind the walls, the prison was three floors high and divided into three discrete areas. The debtors' prison held 100, as did the women's prison, where there were also state apartments. Between the two was the felons' prison, which now held 300 men. Each was built around its own courtyard to allow for exercise and fresh air. There was a chapel, indoor toilets on each of the three floors, taprooms, a coffee room, lodges for the turnkeys and, for the first time, an infirmary. The condemned cells built in 1726 were considered still fit for purpose and were incorporated into the design. It was a vast improvement on the old Newgate.

Akerman felt the new gaol was bigger and airier than before and there was less illness. An illustration of the Marshalsea infirmary from about the same time shows a room with a long platform running most of its length with hammocks suspended above it. Men lie on the ground, the platform and in the hammocks and it's probable that the wards at Newgate were arranged in much the same way. The separate division of masters and common side continued in each of the three sections of the gaol.

The reformer John Howard had been agitating for change, but he does not appear to have been consulted on the improvements to the new gaol. However, between 1777 and 1782, as research for his book *The State of the Prisons in England and Wales,* he managed to get inside for a look:

'The cells built in Old Newgate a few years since for the condemned malefactors are still used for the same purpose. I shall therefore give some account of them. There are upon each of the three floors, five; all vaulted, near nine feet to the crown. Those on the ground floor measure a full 9 feet by near 6; the five on the first story are a little larger (9½ by 6) on account of the set-off in the wall; and the five uppermost, still a little larger for the same reason. In the upper part of each cell, is a window double grated, near 3 feet by 1½. The doors are 4 inches thick. The strong stone wall is lined round each cell with planks, studded with broad-headed nails. In each cell is a barrack bedstead. I was told by those who attended them, that criminals who had affected an air of boldness during their trial, and appeared quite unconcerned at the pronouncing of sentence upon them, were struck with horror, and shed tears, when brought to these dark solitary abodes.'

Though the gaol was clean, free of offensive odours and 'many inconveniences of the old gaol are avoided in this one', Howard couldn't help feeling that, 'it has some manifest errors. It is now too late to point out particulars. All I say is that without more than Ordinary care, the prisoners in it will be in great danger of gaol fever'.

In 1779 there were 1,500 prisoners in London gaols of which 945 were in for debt, a ratio that is probably also applicable to previous centuries. A census taken on 16 August 1779 revealed Newgate contained fifty-one debtors and 141 felons, which was obviously well below its capacity. In 1782, this had risen, according to Howard, to 291 prisoners of whom sixty-six were women. Over a hundred were transports, eighty-nine were being held against payment of fines, twenty-one were under sentence of death and the rest were awaiting trial. The infirmary was near the condemned cells and the cells for the refractory were under the chapel.

A table of fees were set out on a board and nailed to the wall in the yard and Howard duly made a note.

NEWGATE UNDER AKERMAN – A TABLE OF FEES –
from The Life of John Howard Esq

GAOLER: Richard Akerman

Salary: £200

[with fees this averaged out at £800 per annum -
but he had to pay the turnkeys and other staff from this]

Fees: Debtors: 8s 10d
Felons: 18s 10d
Misdemeanours/Fines: 14s 10d
Transports: 14s 10d
Licence: Beer and Wine

PRISONERS

Allowance: Debtors and felons: a penny loaf a day

Garnish: Debtors: 5s 6d
Felons: 2s 6d

CHAPLAIN: Rev Mr Villette
Sunday twice, every day prayers

Salary: £35, etc

SURGEON: Mr Olney

Salary: £50 for all prisoners

Prisoners on the masters side pay 3s entrance fee plus 3d for a room and bedding if they are prepared to share with one other. They pay 2s 6d for their own room. Debtors' discharging fee is 6s 10d.

The prisoners can pay the turnkeys 2s – no other charges on pain of civil action.

He also noted that through the keeper's benevolence, they received a penny loaf (about 8 ounces) a day to eat.

'Etc' against the chaplain's salary probably relates to earnings from the Accounts of the Ordinary of Newgate, a series of books detailing the stories of the condemned men recorded just before they were due to hang and published on death. It made several chaplains, particularly Paul Lorrain who first came up with the idea of selling them, very wealthy. It is also interesting to note that he has had a pay rise and is now paid £35 a year for his services as opposed to £15 in the previous century.

John Howard thought the dejection of spirits observed by Akerman came from a change in circumstances, a poor diet and from the close offensive dungeons where the prisoners were kept eighteen hours out of twenty-four in the noxious filth of their own bodies, and with nothing to occupy them but drinking and gambling. In 1777 and 1792 there were riots in the new gaol.

With the new prison building came a new desire to keep it clean. Richard Akerman was keen and so was Sir Stephen Janssen whose campaign had led to George Dance's commission. Janssen even published a pamphlet in which he recommended that each prisoner should be disinfected with vinegar before attending court to stop, as he'd seen in 1750, gaol fever and other contagious diseases being brought into the courtroom and infecting the officials. As part of this campaign. he also suggested that each felon should have his own cell, a clean shirt every week and that the prison should also be washed down with vinegar to disinfect it.

Turnkeys and Old Bailey officials were issued with a copy of Peter Lanyard's *Directions To Prevent The Contagion Of The Gaol Distemper Commonly Called Gaol Fever* which set out recipes for cleaning products, washes and fumigants to keep the prison clean and free of disease. These little books were carried by turnkeys until the end of the century but there is no evidence the recipes worked. John Howard believed that faith, temperance and cleanliness were proof against gaol fever and the recipes were probably about as effective.

Recipes from Peter Lanyard's book:

'For treating gaol fever:

'Candied orange or lemon peel, preserved ginger, garlic, if not disagreeable, cardamom, caraway may be very useful.

'Should the mouth be clammed, dry raisins, currants, lemon drops will cool and quench the thirst which should it increase, may be assuaged by small draughts of old hock and water, or a small [weak] punch.

'Smelling to good wine vinegar during the trials will not only refresh but revive more agreeably and coolly than spiritous waters distilled from lavender or rosemary.'

'Tobacco stalks and dried herbs – mint, rosemary, southern wood' and 'bruised juniper berries' were to be burned by means of large braziers, pans or coppers. These would mingle with the acrid stench of 'wet gunpowder and frankincense' heaped on 'hot shovels' while steams of hot vinegar were conveyed to all parts of the building. Tar was also burned in the yard while the court was sitting. Vinegar was used as a disinfectant to wash down the prison and the prisoners.

Repellent salves were available at herbalists' shops, which could be rubbed into the stone to keep lice away. None of this effort went down well with the prisoners, but at least the authorities were making an effort in the new place.

Despite Richard Akerman's enlightened insistence on cleanliness, by the end of the century Newgate and its inmates, on the common side at least, were in a filthy neglected state once more. The problem with keeping a gaol clean is that it will keep filling with people. Visitors noted the mentally ill as well as ragged half-naked 'poorer females, particularly convicts, crowded like sheep in a pen'. 'Convict' by now was the term applied to those sentenced to transportation, prisoners were those sentenced to a prison term, and the condemned were those sentenced to die, though they were still all held together in the goal with those awaiting trial.

In 1780, attempts to make prisoners wear a prison uniform were strongly resisted and in 1784 there was an attempt at classifying prisoners, which was greeted in the same manner.

By June 1779 the building was nearly complete. The final touches were a covered passage for the judges and a piazza for a coach stand outside the main gate, but before they could be added the building burned down in one of the worst cases of civil unrest this country as ever seen.

The Gordon Riots of June 1780 were the culmination of opposition to Catholic reforms that had begun in 1778 and gathered momentum over the next two years. In 1779, the opposition organised itself into the Protestant Association under the leadership of Lord Gordon. He was 29, and an MP, so fanatical that even his own family thought he was off his head. He made such a nuisance agitating for the repeal of the Catholic reforms that the king, tired of having his ear bent, refused to receive him. Parliament too had had enough, but Gordon was impervious. He drew up a petition for parliament and announced that he and his supporters would deliver it on 2 June. On that morning he and some 50-60,000 protesters gathered in St George's Fields in Southwark and prepared to march on Westminster. Not all supported his cause; some of the marchers had their own grievances, for example, poor pay and bad working conditions. Some were poor, some better off, some wore their Sunday best. There were banners and bands playing music adding to the carnival atmosphere. Drink was taken. Some of the marchers went the long way round over London Bridge and through the City, others took the shorter route across Westminster Bridge.

When they arrived at parliament, Gordon duly went inside and delivered his petition, but parliament refused to receive it. The crowd was incensed and, with no one willing to read the Riot Act and compel its dispersal, rioting broke out across London that grew quickly out of the control of the constables and even the militia. That evening, the Sardinian ambassador's house and private chapel were destroyed and looted and the 84-year-old Lord Mansfield, the Lord Chief Justice was hauled out of his carriage and beaten up before being rescued by other peers. For four days, the City, which was not unsympathetic to the Protestant Association and which liked to see the Westminster authorities squirm, sat back and did nothing while the government dithered and the rioting escalated. The Lord Mayor, Brackley Kennett, a former waiter and brothel keeper, declared faux-innocently: 'The whole mischief seems to be that the mob have got hold of some people and some furniture they do not like and are burning them, and what is the harm in that?'

Writing to his friend Dr Burney, the Rev Thomas Twining complained about the lack of action and the failure of the City to intervene, 'Civil power? What civil power? A power that will be as civil to the mob as the Lord Mayor was?'

By the fourth day, the rioting was out of control. The streets were not safe, as bands of marauding men ransacked buildings and attacked Catholics. Thousands of rioters gathered back at St George's Fields, but this time they were armed with 'poleaxes, cutlasses and bludgeons'. They set off again this time for 4 Bow Street, the home and office of the 'blind beak' John Fielding where they looted the house, throwing all the contents and thirty years of criminal records into the street and burning them.

The next stop was the prisons, symbols of state oppression where many of their fellow rioters were by now languishing. Some of the rioters passed by the grocer's shop owned by the black writer Ignatius Sancho, who wrote:

'There is at this moment at least 100,000 poor, miserable, ragged rabble, from 12 to 60 years of age, with blue cockades in their hats ... ready for any and every mischief ... There is about a thousand mad men armed with clubs, bludgeons and crows, just now set off for Newgate, to liberate they say, their honest comrades.'

At 7pm they arrived at the brand-new Newgate, which had been widely considered impregnable because of its high, thick stone walls. In the vanguard of the mob were two free men, called John Glover and Benjamin Bowsey, described in contemporary newspaper reports as 'black' or 'mulatto'.

The weak point was the keeper's house in the centre where Richard Akerman lived with his family and servants. Unlike the rest of the gaol which was constructed of stone it was made of brick and had windows. When Akerman refused to surrender his prison, the rioters took their mattocks, sledgehammers, pickaxes and crowbars and stormed the house. Akerman, his family, servants and turnkeys fled over the rooftops, while the rioters threw his belongings into the street, burned them and set fire to the house.

It was soon blazing out of control, and was stoked and added to until it had spread throughout the gaol. The heat was so intense that stones of two to three tons were razed, some of them vitrified, and the iron window bars buckled and melted. The vast pall of smoke could be seen rising high into the summer-evening sky.

Meanwhile the resourceful rioters produced ladders which they laid against the walls and, shouting and yelling in triumph, they climbed up to rescue the terrified screaming prisoners hauling them up by their legs and hair. In the street they struck off their irons as the flames roared, the stones crashed and the iron bars of the gaol expanding in the heat clanged and bonged around them. The poet George Crabbe witnessed the whole thing and afterward wrote in an account:

'I went close to it, and never saw anything so dreadful. The prison was a remarkably strong building, but, determined to force it, they broke the gates with crows and other instruments, and climbed up outside the cell part, which joins the two great wings of the building where the felons were confined; they broke the roof, tore away the rafters, and having got ladders, they descended. Not Orpheus himself had more courage or better luck. Flames all around them, and a body of soldiers expected, yet they defied and laughed at all opposition. The prisoners escaped. I stood and saw about twelve women and eight men ascend from their confinement to the open air, and they were conducted through the streets in their chains. Three of these were to be hanged on Friday.'

Around one hundred constables did arrive to try and restore order, but the streets had been sealed by the rioters and they were beaten off, their truncheons set on fire and thrown as firebrands into the gaol. Three other City gaols were attacked that night, including the Clink which was falling down anyway and therefore almost empty; it was never rebuilt. At the Clerkenwell compter, the prisoners were released and the buildings left standing, while at the Fleet the debtors were allowed to collect their belongings and leave before it too was torched. It was rebuilt in 1781-2 and finally closed in 1846. The two Southwark gaols, the King's Bench and the Marshalsea were also attacked. Many of the prisoners who escaped that night were never recaptured.

The rioters, by now well-fuelled with beer, spirits and neat alcohol looted from breweries and distilleries, then marched on the Bank of England but the government, militia and City authorities had finally rallied and placed 12,000 troops on the streets giving the soldiers orders to fire on all groups of four or more men. Over the next day, which became known as Black Wednesday, 285 people were killed with 200 wounded. The total death toll, however, is unknown since others died of alcohol poisoning and many more died at home of their wounds. Around 450 were arrested, ninety-six of these, some no more than children, were tried at the Old Bailey for rioting but acquitted. Thirty-five were sentenced to death but in the end only twenty-four were hanged. Glover and Bowsey who had been captured and sent to Newgate were reprieved. One of those condemned was the then hangman Edward Dennis who had been in the thick of the action. He appealed and as part of the petition requested his son be appointed hangman in his place. Luckily for them both his appeal succeeded.

There is no death toll for the Newgate prisoners that night and it thought that they all escaped - even the condemned. Their irons were struck off in the street and many got clean away, though not all.

The next day Samuel Johnson and his friend Dr Scott joined the sightseers at the still smouldering ruins: a brave move considering the riots were still raging.

> 'As I went by the Protestants were plundering the sessions house at the Old Bailey. They were not I believe, a hundred, but they did their work at leisure, in full security, without sentinels, without trepidation, as men lawfully employed, in a full day.'

Prisoners, too, drifted back over the next few days, some out of curiosity, some, pathetically, because they had nowhere else to go. Some, according to Dickens writing in Barnaby Rudge some sixty years after the event 'were being often found asleep in the ruins or sitting talking there or even eating or drinking as in a choice retreat'. They were all re-arrested and sent to the compters. The prison was rebuilt over the next three years at a cost of £30,000 and Richard Akerman retained his position as keeper. He was praised for his courage in trying to reason with the mob. Writing afterwards about the riots, some of the worst this country's ever seen, his friend and admirer James Boswell referred to him as 'my esteemed friend Mr Akerman, the keeper of Newgate, who long discharged a very important trust with a uniform intrepid firmness and at the same time a tenderness and liberal charity, which enables him to be recorded with distinguished honour.'

Gordon was arrested for treason and sent to the Tower. He was acquitted at his trial in 1781 and went abroad. When he returned several years later, it was as an Orthodox Jew. But he couldn't help himself. In 1787 he was sentenced to five years for publishing libels. He was unable to get bail and died, somewhat ironically in Newgate, of typhus in 1793.

TYBURN

It has been estimated by the contemporary statistician Patrick Colquhoun that at the end of the eighteenth century, 63,000 people supported 'themselves in or near the metropolis by pursuits either criminal, illegal, or immoral' at a time when the population of London was under a million.

Between 1740 and 1799, 1,696 men and women were executed in London and Middlesex. Numbers varied from year to year and could be as few as six or as many as 108. Between 1749 and 1754 and again from 1764 to 1787 over fifty a year were executed. This was at the height of the Bloody Code, and although the courts did their best to mitigate the charges by undervaluing the goods stolen or permitting a defendant to plead benefit of the clergy, they could not, and would not, save everyone. A large number of the death sentences, around sixty per cent, were also commuted, usually to transportation, or pardoned. In 1688 there were fifty capital crimes but over the eighteenth century the number rose until by 1815 there were 288. These included stealing goods worth five shillings or more, impersonating a Chelsea Pensioner and cutting down a tree.

From the early nineteenth century and into the 1830s, thanks to the campaigns of the penal reformers, capital crimes for civilians were reduced until by 1861 only murder, treason, espionage, piracy with violence and arson in the Royal Dockyards remained. Of the records of 49,000 crimes tried at the Old Bailey that still exist, ninety-five per cent are to do with property. The victims of the majority of these crimes would have been the poor. The rest were physical assaults including murder. The story of Mary Young, the leader of a gang of pickpockets and thieves, is typical.

Mary Young was born, according to the ordinary's account, in Ireland around 1704 and trained to be a needlewoman, but she had an 'itching desire' to see London. She achieved her dream aged about fifteen, but it wasn't all it was cracked up to be since she quickly became a prostitute and petty thief.

In 1738, she was arrested and tried for pickpocketing. It was her second offence, but she gave a false name and was tried as a first time offender. Instead of being hanged, she was transported to Virginia, but she didn't stay long, making her way back to England after bribing the captain of a returning ship. It was an action that would have ended in the death penalty had she been caught. By 1740 she was back to thieving again, running a gang of men and women who specialised in theft, distraction and giving false evidence and operated around London Bridge and the Royal Exchange. Like other London thieves, they enjoyed a lucrative day out at the races and followed the crowds to a fair. She was nicknamed Jenny Diver after the prostitute-pickpocket in *The Beggar's Opera*.

Mary was a resourceful fearless woman, and a mistress of disguise. A favourite was a fake belly with hands and arms folded across it and her own arms and hands hidden inside. When a likely mark turned up, she was able to steal their goods without appearing to move. The swell of her belly also served as a handy cache for the loot. She was extremely successful and lived in some style in Covent Garden with a maid, her lover and their young daughter who was about three when her mother died.

She was arrested in January 1741 along with an accomplice Elizabeth Davies after attempting to steal a purse from another woman. A second, male, accomplice got away. This time there was no escape. She tried to plead the belly in the hope of reprieve, but it was clearly a lie. And she was sentenced to hang on 18 March 1741.

'On this day twenty-two were due to hang, including Mary, but two died in the condemned cells. Of the remaining twenty, sixteen were men - three burglars, eight robbers, two horse thieves, a sheep-stealer, a forger and a returned transport. Two of the women had robbed a countryman and a brothel, one was a house-breaker and the last Mary Young, who was also known as Jenny Diver, for street robbery.'

When the noose was put around her neck at Newgate for the journey to Tyburn she was said to be very shocked and she died begging for favourable treatment in the afterlife. Elizabeth Davies was transported.

In 1759 the triple tree, the triangular structure that could hang twenty-four people at a time had been replaced with a moveable gallows that could be dismantled after each hanging day and also set up at other sites. The new gallows introduced the 'sudden drop', which broke the neck ensuring a quicker death than the slow strangulation that resulted from being pushed off a cart. And the boiled heads of traitors continued to be put up on spikes at Temple Bar for most of the century.

On the whole, women were opportunist thieves, stealing generally from fellow lodgers, empty yards or open windows while men tended to steal from the person or break into houses. They stole goods in transit, sugar from the quays and coal from the warehouses, and rustled livestock and fancy dogs. They robbed the pubs of their pewter tankards and hauled corpses out of graves to sell to the physicians for dissection.

They also engaged in coining and counterfeiting coin, both of which carried the death penalty for the impact it had on the economy. Counterfeiters generally forged the small coinage such as farthings and halfpennies as it was easier and less noticeable. Coiners clipped tiny bits of gold or silver from higher value coins. At a time when money was still made of precious metal and the weight of each coin was integral to its value any reduction in weight devalued the coin and so undermined the economy since often the clippings would be melted together and used as currency. This crime was also harsher on the poor since the rich wouldn't suffer greatly from a clipped coin, but a poor person might starve when a forged coin was refused.

Among the cruellest tricks of the fraudster was to offer to use influence they didn't have to obtain a pardon for a condemned man. The poor victim who would be prepared to do anything to save his life would often be taken in.

The young James Boswell loved an execution and went with his friend George Selwyn to as many as he could, getting as close as possible. 'I got upon the scaffold very near the fatal tree ... and I was most terribly shocked and thrown into a very deep melancholy,' he noted in 1769, but it didn't stop him. Twenty years later, however it was all a bit old hat 'this morning I saw three men hanged at Newgate,' he wrote as an afterthought in a letter to a friend.

Boswell was attending an execution at Newgate not Tyburn because, in November 1783, hangings were moved to a triangular patch of land at the top of Old Bailey outside the recently-completed debtor's prison. The gallows were a new design with a trapdoor in the floor through which the condemned person fell in an attempt to break their necks. It was not always successful. The first hanging was on 9 December 1783, when a vast crowd of people crammed into the street to watch nine men and one woman hang. And at the hanging of three forgers in June 1798, an estimated 100,000 men and women, rich and poor, turned out to enjoy the day. As well as thronging the streets, they climbed onto rooftops, and crowded out of windows.

There were around ten hanging days a year either at Tyburn, before 1783, or after that date at the newly reconstructed Newgate, when a scaffold was erected on the Sunday night while the condemned were in chapel. The last man to be hanged at Tyburn was John Austin, a highwayman, on 3 November 1783.

At Newgate, it was still the custom for the condemned to make a final speech. Some were very short, just a mumbled apology and some thanks. Others used it as an opportunity to defy the authorities and stir the crowd who egged them on. Some others made long windy speeches in the hope of a last-minute reprieve.

Despite the lengths the courts went to not to apply the death penalty, and unease over the way it could be applied to minor crimes, the debate of its abolition did not surface until the end of the century. Prior to that the question was rather over whether it should carried out in public or private.

The magistrate and author Henry Fielding thought executions would appear much more terrible and therefore have a greater deterrent value if carried out in private. Johnson and Boswell, on the other hand, could not see any harm in an event that gave so much enjoyment to the public and supported the condemned through their final hours. Johnson was disappointed when the execution site moved east and the processions to Tyburn stopped, but he need not have worried, the crowds simply moved to stand outside Newgate on a hanging day.

Burning continued until 1789 when Catherine Murphy was the last woman to be burned at the stake; her crime was coining. She was convicted with eight others, including her husband Hugh, who as men, were sentenced to hang on 18 September. In keeping with the custom, the Sheriff of London Sir Benjamin Hammett, had requested she should be strangled before the fire was lit. She was executed after the men and had to walk past their swinging bodies to the stake where she was placed on a foot-high, ten-inch square platform and secured with ropes and an iron ring. When she had finished her prayers, the faggots were piled around her and the platform removed so she dropped and was strangled. After half an hour the fire was lit.

Hammett used Murphy's execution as an example when he pressed for the ending of burning as a punishment. It was abolished the following year in the Treason Act 1790.

In the sixteenth century, when Henry VIII was boiling his prisoners alive, executioners were known as 'William Boilman'. By the end of the seventeenth, they were known as Jack Ketch after the famously incompetent incumbent. Executioners came from a variety of backgrounds; some were butchers, evidently because of their ability to take life and their knowledge of dead bodies, others might be former prisoners. In 1715, the executioner got £3 for beheading a peer and the same for hanging, drawing and quartering a gentleman. He was also allowed to keep any clothes worn by the victims, any money in the pockets and any bribes he might be offered to make the end quick. In 1715, John Thrift planned to invest his earnings from executing seventy or so Jacobite rebels, not only in 'the title of an esquire, but the estate too'. In 1763, the hangman got more than he bargained for when a fearsome Irishwoman called Hannah Dagoe refused to go quietly. After almost knocking him out she tore off nearly all her clothes and flung them into the crowd so he couldn't sell them, then tying a handkerchief over her face she leapt off the cart with the noose about her neck with such force she broke her neck instantly.

William Brunskill, the hangman from 1786-1814 was credited with 537 executions at Newgate alone.

The Royal College of Physicians was entitled to ten bodies a year as were the Royal College of Surgeons, St Thomas's and St Bart's. And there are records in the accounts of the Royal College of Surgeons of payments to the beadles who collected the bodies and for a Christmas box of 2s 6d to the hangman.

There were four dissections a year at the Barber-Surgeons Hall in nearby Wood Street using male and female bodies and huge crowds gathered despite the fact that dissection was seen as a further punishment since it prevented the soul going to Heaven. On at least one occasion though the 'corpse' was not actually dead. In 1740 William Duell, a robber, came round on the table. Once he had recovered, he was transported.

William Hunter the eminent eighteenth century anatomist and physician took things one stage further. In 1776, he commissioned the Italian artist Agostina Carlini to make him an écorché figure (that is sculpted without skin so the musculature is exposed) of a man posed in imitation of an ancient Roman sculpture known as the Dying Gaul. The body of a suitably muscular criminal was selected from the range on offer at Tyburn and the corpse duly flayed and cast in plaster and then bronze. While the bronze has been lost, the plaster casts and some of Carlini's drawings survive. The identity of the subject is not known, but since he was thought to have been a smuggler, the bronze was called, mockingly,

Smugglerius. It is possible that he was Thomas Henman or Benjamin Harley who were sentenced to be executed dissected and anatomised for murdering a customs officer, however research in 2010 has tentatively identified Smugglerius as James Langar, a footpad who was hanged on 12 April 1776.

The job of prison chaplain in a gaol such as Newgate was dangerous and pretty thankless. Apart from the smell, the risk of disease and the occupational hazards of lice and fleas, there was the attitude of the prisoners, no respecters of authority, who may or may not have had any time for religion. Apart from the funeral service, which the condemned men were obliged to attend, going to chapel was not compulsory. There were a few dedicated souls who attended chapel regularly, while others came to heckle and cheek the chaplain. But many others used their Sunday mornings to play football and hang out in the yard. Often the chaplains would have to shout their sermons over the racket made by the congregation, who thought nothing of eating, drinking and spitting during the service and even 'urinating in the corner'. In 1719, a prisoner smuggled in a dirty magazine and the service had to be halted. After two Bibles were stolen, their replacements were chained as in medieval times. It was a battle of wills.

John Howard attended several chapel services at Newgate as research for his report on *The State of the Prisons in England*. He wrote

'The chapel is plain and neat. Below is the chaplain's seat, and three of four pews for the felons; that in the centre is for the condemned. On each side is a gallery that for the women is towards their ward; in it is a pew for the keeper, whose presence may set a good example and be otherwise useful. The other gallery towards the debtors ward is for them. The stairs to each gallery are on the outside of the chapel. I attended there several times, and Mr Villette said the prayers distinctly and with propriety: the prisoners who were present, seemed attentive; but we were disturbed by noise in the court. Surely they who will not go to chapel, who are by far the greater number, should be locked up in their rooms during the time of divine service and not suffered to hinder the edification of such as are better disposed.'

In the eighteenth century, when it became popular, particularly among the well-to-do, to attend the Sunday and funeral services and view the condemned who sat round a coffin, the debtors had to stay behind in their wards due to the lack of space. Naturally, the turnkeys charged entry to the chapel and, in 1729, it was estimated that on a good day they could make £20.

Ten ordinaries served Newgate over the course of the eighteenth century. They lived in a house in Newgate Street that came with the job and the received a salary of £35 a year. To boost this income, they started up sidelines, for example, at the beginning of the century John Allen ran a funeral service. But the most popular and the most lucrative was publishing the accounts they took from the condemned prisoners and selling them on the day of execution, even at Tyburn. These ran alongside the *Proceedings of the Old Bailey* as a kind of sister publication.

Over 200 of these accounts still exist, though many perished as the speed with which they were published meant they were often of very poor quality. The format was pretty standard. There was an account of the trial, followed by a description of the crimes, the condemned person's confessions and a lurid description of the execution. They cost around tuppence but could fetch as much as sixpence if the prisoner was famous or the confessions particularly juicy.

The earliest accounts were by Samuel Smith who was the ordinary between 1676 and 1698 but it was the eighteenth century ordinaries who showed the greatest resource. Paul Lorrain, who held the post from 1700 to1719, was the first to start publishing and selling them and often his accounts would include advertisements. In 1744, James Guthrie, the ordinary from 1734 to 1746, added long appendices. After 1745, attention was focused on the lurid details of the crimes and trials of the condemned rather than their confessions. The intended purpose of the accounts was to teach people the wages of sin.

The prisoners were not always that keen to be immortalised in print, so the ordinaries would offer inducements for them to spill the beans. The enterprising John Allen offered to recommend reprieves in exchange for the confessions. The ordinaries guarded the privilege to publish these accounts very jealously and resented anything that interfered with their production and sale, from prisoners who refused to cooperate to journalists such as the frequently hard-up Daniel Defoe, who occasionally published rival accounts, thus depleting the pool of profits.

On one occasion the ordinary John Villette was serving at Tyburn when the young boy who was about to hang got a reprieve. Villette, with an eye on his profits, told the executioner to go ahead anyway. The man refused and the boy was spared.

Increasing competition and a decline in the demand for this kind of reading spelled the end of the Ordinary's Accounts. John Villette, ordinary between 1774 and 1799, published the last volume in 1777.

After this the *Newgate Calendar*, also known as the *Malefactor's Bloody Register*, was published. It was historically selective and featured the most famous and notorious cases across the eighteenth century. It ran from 1773 to 1826.

John Howard, born in 1726, was the son of a prosperous upholsterer who inherited a large estate at the age of eighteen. His mother had died when he was five and his father had him sent away to school where he grew up to be a quiet, kind, serious young man with a strong Calvinist faith. He was unhappily apprenticed to a grocer but he left when his father died and, like many young men of his time, went travelling. He returned and after a brief marriage to a lady thirty years his senior, he set off in 1755 for Portugal. En route his ship, the *Hanover*, was captured by the French pirates and he was held prisoner in Brest for six days before he was freed in a prisoner exchange. It is thought that this experience sparked his interest in prison conditions. On his release, he set about helping his fellow prisoners of war. He settled on his estate in Bedfordshire where he was good landlord, improving conditions for his tenants and paying for the education of their children. In 1758, he married Henrietta Leeds, who died in 1765 giving birth to a son, also called John, who was to die 34 years later in an asylum. In 1773, aged 47, John Howard became High Sheriff of Bedfordshire and part of his role was to oversee Bedford Gaol. It changed his life. His concern for the conditions he found in Bedford led him to travel across Britain and Europe looking into the treatment of prisoners and publishing his findings. He was particularly appalled that some prisoners who had been found innocent of all the charges against them continued to be held in prison after their acquittal because they could not afford to pay their exit fees. He suggested abolishing the fees and paying the keeper a salary, but this was rejected on grounds of cost.

He continued travelling and reporting on prisons and in 1774 his evidence led to the Gaol Act, which abolished the exit charge thus freeing innocent prisoners immediately on acquittal and which authorised improvements to prison conditions. He paid for copies of the Act to be printed and sent to every gaol in the country where they were largely ignored. In 1777, he published *The State of the Prisons in England and Wales, With Some Account of Foreign Prisons*, and he visited the new Newgate as part of his research.

In the report he recommended clean accommodation and clothing, proper health care - both physical and mental, a good diet and adequate clean water, segregation of prisoners according to gender, the seriousness of the offence and mental capacity. He suggested abolishing the practice of ironing prisoners and introduced the revolutionary idea of getting prisoners to work which would keep them occupied while in gaol and help them find a job on release, though these weren't adopted until after his death. Not all his ideas were good, however, since he also advocated keeping prisoners in isolation.

By 1784, Howard calculated that he had travelled 42,000 miles (68,000km) visiting prisons and although not all his recommendations were taken up, his work was recognised in numerous awards and freedoms including the Freedom of the City of London.

Howard died in 1790, with cruel irony, of typhus, a disease about which he had long tried to raise awareness, after visiting a prison in what is now Ukraine and he is buried out there.

John Howard was the first person to carry out a thorough investigation into the state of prisons. His ideas were a huge influence on the reformer Jeremy

Bentham but were opposed by Elizabeth Fry who, while agreeing on the need for work, believed in the value of prisoner association. The Howard Association, founded in 1866, was named in his honour; today, as the Howard League for Penal Reform it is Britain's biggest penal reform organisation.

NEWGATE INMATES

Three prisoners who caused a sensation at the time of their arrest were a political agitator, spy and novelist, a petty thief turned master escapologist and a wicked murderess.

Daniel Defoe

Before he became a famous novelist, Daniel Defoe was an English merchant, journalist, especially of economic journalism of which he was a pioneer, pamphleteer and spy.

He was born Daniel Foe (he added the 'De' later to sound posh) around 1660, the son of a prosperous London tallow merchant. Originally he was destined for life in the Presbyterian Ministry, but on completing his education, Defoe decided to become a merchant. He loved trade and was on the whole very good at it, but there were times when he was plagued by misfortune and in 1692 went bankrupt owing £17,000. He was imprisoned for debt but within ten years had repaid all but £5,000. Nevertheless, his fortunes continued to fluctuate throughout his life and he wrote of himself:

'No man has tasted differing fortunes more,

And thirteen times I have been rich and poor.'

Defoe was, by his own admission, impetuous, rash and may not always have been over-scrupulous in his dealings. He was married to Mary for nearly 50 years, and she bore him eight children, six of whom survived to adulthood. Although not much is known of Mary, her calm devotion appears to have been a good balance to her husband's impulsiveness.

Defoe, a dissenter, also had a keen interest in politics, to which trade and religion were closely tied, though his allegiances were somewhat fluid. His first political pamphlets started appearing in 1683 and they were a thorn in the government and the king's sides, and both parties began to see Defoe as a dangerous radical.

In 1703 he was imprisoned for seditious libel after anonymously publishing *The Shortest Way With Dissenters* a pamphlet attacking both High-Church Conservative politicians and low-church dissenters in public office. It was not long before the author's name became public and the advert for his arrest described him unflatteringly as 'a middle-size spare man, about 40 years old, of a brown complexion, and dark-brown coloured hair, but wears a wig, a hooked nose, a sharp chin, grey eyes, and a large mole near his mouth'. Defoe was not impressed. He was tried at the Old Bailey and advised to plead guilty and rely on the court's mercy. It was poor advice. He was fined heavily and sentenced to stand three times in the pillory. While waiting for his sentence to be carried out, Defoe, though anxious about the impending ordeal wrote the poem *Hymn To The Pillory* which snatched some kind of victory from the jaws of defeat. When placed in the pillory, the notoriously partisan crowd, cheered him and drank his health. Instead of dead cats and faeces, they threw flowers and offered him wine to drink from a sponge. Copies of *Hymn To The Pillory* sold like hot cakes. Defoe's biographer John Robert Moore later wrote that 'no man in England but Defoe ever stood in the pillory and later rose to eminence among his fellow men'.

However, there was still the matter of the fine. As Defoe languished in Newgate unable to pay, his tile business at Tilbury collapsed leaving him concerned for the welfare of his wife and large family. He appealed to his friend Robert Harley, the Earl of Oxford, who brokered a deal with the Tory government releasing Defoe on the condition that he would become their pamphleteer and secret agent.

On release from Newgate, Defoe continued to ricochet through life. Aged 59, he started a new career as a novelist, his most famous book might be *Robinson Crusoe*, but *Moll Flanders* is set in Newgate and the heroine speaks of poverty as 'a frightful spectre'. In later years, Defoe's health failed and it is thought that when he died on 24 April, 1731 he was in hiding from his creditors.

Jack Sheppard

Jack Sheppard was born in Spitalfields in 1702. He was apprenticed to be a carpenter like his father, and after a series of bad breaks when one master died and another mistreated him, he began to show real promise. He was small, 5ft 4in (1.63m) and slight with huge dark eyes and a slight stutter. He was deceptively strong, extremely witty and very popular, particularly with the ladies. But in 1722 he turned to crime, apparently after falling in with his buxom prostitute girlfriend, Elizabeth Lyon known as Edgeworth Bess, whom he met at the Black Lion in Drury Lane while indulging in another of his passions, strong drink.

His speciality, though he doesn't seem to have been especially good at it, was housebreaking and it wasn't long before he fell in with Jonathan Wild and his gang and became further embroiled in the criminal underworld. When Bess was arrested and imprisoned in St Giles's Roundhouse, Sheppard, angry that wasn't allowed to visit, broke in and rescued her.

In February 1724, Sheppard's brother Tom, also carpenter and a thief, was arrested for a burglary he, Sheppard and Bess had committed in Clare Market. Fearing that he would be hanged, Tom grassed on his brother and Jack was arrested thanks to a tip-off from the thief-taker Jonathan Wild, who pocketed a £40 reward. Sheppard was imprisoned on the top floor of the St Giles Roundhouse pending further questioning but escaped using a rope made of his bedclothes. Still wearing his irons, he joined the crowd that had been drawn by the noise of his escape. To aid his getaway, he pointed to shadows on the roof claiming he could see a man hiding there, then he legged it.

On 19 May he was arrested again, this time for pickpocketing in Leicester Fields. He ended up with Bess in the New Prison in Clerkenwell, but within a week they had filed through their manacles, escaped through a window by removing a bar, climbed over the gate of the next-door bridewell and fled. After this, his reputation as a popular hero began to grow.

Sheppard turned down an offer to work again with Jonathan Wild, teaming up instead with a burglar known as Joseph 'Blueskin' Blake, but he had made a dangerous enemy in Wild, who informed on him to the authorities. Sheppard was arrested and put in Newgate to await trial. He was convicted on 12 August and sentenced to hang on 4 September but he loosened a bar in a window and escaped in women's clothes smuggled into Newgate for him by Bess. He hid out of town for a few days but it seems he could not stay away. He returned to London and was arrested on 9 September, where he was again sent to Newgate until a hanging day came round. After a further foiled attempt at escape he was imprisoned, fettered hand and foot, in a secure cell high in the Newgate gatehouse called 'the Castle', which was considered the strongest room in the prison. His fetters were stapled to the floor and secured with a large padlock, but even that could not hold him.

On 15 October, he freed his wrists from his cuffs, picked the padlock with a nail, broke his fetters by twisting the weakest link, tied the chains to his legs with rags and with the heavy padlock, smashed the fireplace. In the chimney he found a bar that had been wedged across to prevent escapes. Removing it, he climbed the flue in to the room above the Castle, which was unused, and picked the lock of its door to find himself in a corridor leading to the chapel. He used the iron bar to break through the stone wall into the chapel, and after picking the locks of two more doors, he levered a third off its hinges to find himself on the gatehouse roof. With no way of lowering himself down onto the roof of the nextdoor house, he had to retrace his steps to his cell where he collected his blanket and returned. He used the blanket to lower himself down onto the roof of the house, forced the window and slipped through into an empty garret. After a short rest, he crept down the stairs and out into Giltspur Street. He made his way west where he found a blacksmith willing to strike his irons.

His astonishing escape was the talk of the town, a triumph for the popular hero, a huge embarrassment for the keeper and his men, but it was to be short-lived. Two weeks later he broke into a pawnbroker's on Drury Lane where he stole a black silk suit, a silver sword, rings, watches and a wig among other things. On 1 November, he was arrested blind drunk and wearing most of the stolen goods at a brandy shop on Drury Lane.

In the fortnight before his hanging, crowds flocked to see him; the going rate payable to the keeper and turnkeys was four shillings though the figure of £200 has also been mentioned. The eminent portrait painter Sir James Thornhill was among those who visited and he sketched Sheppard's portrait.

After attempts to get him to inform on his associates and to have his sentence commuted to transportation, Jack Sheppard was hanged at Tyburn on 16 November 1724; it seems that even on the way to the Tyburn he was planning to cut the ropes that bound him and escape. Owing to his slight build his death by strangulation was long and prolonged and the crowd who'd cheered him on his way to the gallows were horrified.

Sheppard's supporters were determined his body would not fall into the hands of the surgeons and his corpse was taken away on their shoulders but a fight broke out in the crowd when a rumour circulated that the surgeons had got it after all. Eventually Sheppard was taken to a tavern in Long Acre where his friends shared one (or two) last drinks with him. He was eventually laid to rest in the graveyard at St-Martins-in-the-Fields.

Sheppard became a folk hero, he was immortalised as Macheath in The *Beggar's Opera* and the nineteenth century American outlaw Jesse James used his name as a pseudonym.

Elizabeth Brownrigg

Elizabeth Brownrigg was the wife of painter and decorator James Brownrigg who took on two girl apprentices, Mary Clifford and Mary Mitchell, to grind white lead, among other duties, at his premises in Flower-de-Luce Court which linked Fetter Lane with Fleet Street. Both girls were kept nearly naked; Mary Clifford was once seen by a male apprentice wearing nothing but her shoes and stockings and she begged him for something to cover herself with. She was a bed-wetter and so singled out for especially violent treatment by Elizabeth. She was often tied naked to a hook and whipped or she was starved and chained to a door.

One day the baker next door was so alarmed by the cries coming from the house that he sent one of his own workers up onto the roof to see what was going on. Peering through the skylight, the man could see Mary covered in blood and nearly unconscious. Appalled, the baker alerted the authorities and the girls were removed, but not in time to save Mary, who died of her injuries in St Bartholomew's Hospital a few days later. The apothecary, who treated her, told the Old Bailey that 'she was in the most shocking condition. I never saw such a thing in my life'. James Brownrigg was acquitted of murder, but he and his son were found guilty of assaulting Mary Mitchell. They were each fined a shilling and sentenced to six months in Newgate. Elizabeth Brownrigg was hanged at Tyburn on 14 September 1767. The crowd was so great that several people were injured in the crush.

The newspapers at the time noted that, had the clergyman and lay preacher not travelled in the cart with her, Elizabeth would not have reached Tyburn alive. Missiles were thrown at her while the crowd hissed and booed and shouted. It showed their revulsion at the evil treatment of two young girls. Many of the crowd members were, or had been, apprentices.

Chapter 7
Reform
1800 - 1902

When the century turned, Newgate was still London's main prison; it was one of nineteen in the capital and six in the City and for the first twenty-odd years, conditions continued pretty much as they always had. The reforms started in 1806 under the Solicitor General Sir Samuel Romilly, who managed to get the death penalty repealed for theft. In 1817, the new keeper made cooked meat available more than once a week and stopped the practice of ironing. In 1819, the death penalty was repealed for other capital crimes and in 1823, Sir Robert Peel, the Home Secretary, introduced the Gaols Act, which made it permissible for a judge to record a sentence of death in the full knowledge it would not be carried out; it was usually replaced by transportation or service in the army or Royal Navy. Peel served twice as Home Secretary and twice as Prime Minister. In his second term as Home Secretary he instigated the reform for which he is still best known when the Metropolitan Police Force was established by act of parliament. The police officers quickly became known as Bobbies, an affectionate reference to their founder and while they weren't popular they were extremely effective at reducing crime. He also got rid of the old system of gaol fees by making prison officials salaried employees, and backed the reformists' campaign by introducing the education of prisoners.

By the 1830s, only seven per cent of those condemned were executed. The act also attempted to impose uniformity in prisons across the country although this didn't happen until 1877. By 1827, Peel was boasting: 'there is not a single law connected with my name which has not had for its object some mitigation of the criminal law'. He continued removing the death penalty from the statute books during tenures as Prime Minister, briefly in 1834 and again in 1841. Alongside these changes to sentencing came new ideas of penal reform, which developed across the century as debate raged over the best ways of punishing offenders.

But the biggest changes, and the ones that would lead to the reform of the entire prison system, came out of the work done by the Quaker Elizabeth Fry who visited the women's quarters in 1817. She was so appalled at the squalid conditions she found there that she began campaigning to improve their lot, providing work and education for the female inmates and their children. After her intervention, the prisons were cleaner and the prisoners more gainfully employed. One visitor in the 1820s even observed a condemned man studying French grammar.

However, there was a vocal opposition that objected to the pampering of prisoners. The writer and cleric Sydney Smith wanted them to suffer so that on release they should be 'heartily wearied of their residence and taught by sad experience to consider it the greatest misfortune of their lives to attend to it'. What they should 'attend' to, he suggested was 'beating hemp and pulling oakum': that is unpicking tarred rope, a finger-shredding, mind-numbing activity he felt would help them reflect on the error of their ways and stop them reoffending.

From 1834, the Old Bailey sessions house was renamed the Central Criminal Court and its jurisdiction officially extended to cover England and Wales for major trials. Newgate was still the holding prison for those awaiting trial at the Old Bailey, as it was now popularly known, as well as the holding place for those awaiting death and transportation. And of course, it was also the place of execution for those facing capital punishment.

In 1835, there was a newly-appointed inspectorate of prisons who visited Newgate in 1840 and, in spite of all these efforts, reported that the gaol was still 'a great school for crime... prisoners must quit the prison worse than when they first entered it'. The same year, the House of Lords recommended that the controversial Silent System, favoured in the jails of Philadelphia, should be adopted. It worked on the theory that prisoners kept in solitary confinement would reflect on their sins, realise the error of their ways and put their lives of crime behind them, though there were those who recognised that it was more likely to drive men insane. Nevertheless, the wrestling and boxing, the games of football and shove-halfpenny, the newspapers, whoring, drinking, gambling and business activities were stopped and this system of solitary confinement brought in.

As crime proliferated, reformist thinking gathered pace. Over the century, old punishments, such as hanging and the pillory fell out of favour and, alongside transportation, a spell in prison, usually with hard labour, became the sentence most frequently handed down. To meet the demand created by this new sentencing, more jails were needed. Debate raged over the purpose of imprisonment and how best to design and run these new prisons to achieve that purpose.

One idea put forward by the reformer Jeremy Bentham was revolutionary. The panopticon, which he spent sixteen years designing at the end of the eighteenth century, was a circular building constructed round a central watchtower with cells around the perimeter allowing, in theory, all the inmates to be watched all the time. In reality, this constant supervision was not possible but, because of the design, the prisoners had no way of knowing this and therefore had to behave as if they were under continual surveillance. Bentham hoped this prison would be built and that he would be its governor. In the event it was rejected, though the idea of the panopticon was incorporated into the new prisons of the nineteenth century, such as Millbank and Pentonville.

The Millbank Penitentiary, which opened in 1821 and closed in 1903, was the first national, that is, not private, gaol. To meet demand, the new prisons were larger and, since land in town was scarce and expensive, they were built on the edge of London. By the time Newgate, the last of the old prisons closed, there were only five prisons serving the whole of London. Four, Brixton (opened 1820), Pentonville (1842), Wandsworth (1851), Wormwood Scrubs (1891) were for men, while Holloway (1852) was for women. Like Millbank, they were run by the government.

In 1858, the interior of Newgate was reconfigured to give every man his own cell, the masters and common sides vanished forever and the Silent System was brought in with the inmates put to picking oakum and beating hemp. By the end of the century, the prison uniforms that had been so heartily resisted a hundred years earlier were brought in. The heavy shapeless white suits with pillbox hats all printed with broad arrows had originally been used to mark out convicts during transportation but over the 1870s and 1880s, they found their way into domestic prisons. The uniform was worn by men and women. The designations, however, remained the same: those on remand and sentenced to detention were known as prisoners, those sentenced to penal servitude, or transportation were known as convicts.

Although Georgian society ran cheerfully on credit, with many people running accounts, which were settled quarterly, the attitude to debt seems to have changed in the nineteenth century. Levels escalated dramatically and it became very shameful on a personal level. In 1779, of 1,500 prisoners in London's gaols 945 were in for debt. By 1815, it is estimated that 7,000 debtors passed through the doors of Newgate, the Poultry Compter and the Giltspur Street Compter and that at any one time they might hold 1,700 between them, so although George Dance had allocated space for 100 debtors in his new Newgate, the space often held 300-500 people.

In the first half of the nineteenth century, the debtors' side of Newgate was 'a little world within itself - a sort of epitome of London'. To save on rent, or because they had nowhere else to go, the debtors often had their families with them. Dickens, who knew the inside of a debtors' prison as well as anyone, owing to his father's impecuniosity, set several books in the Marshalsea, most notably *Little Dorrit*. As before, some of the debtors might be in prison for years and might even run businesses from there.

For example, at the King's Bench in 1820 there were a cobbler, a barber, circulating libraries, grocers, bakers and cheesemongers - all debtors - who did a thriving trade. At the Fleet, clergymen would provide themselves with an income by offering cut-price weddings and christenings. In addition, there were prostitutes and card sharps always ready to do what they could to feed the debt. Day-to-day life with its privileges for the masters side and charity on the common side operated in much the same way as it did in the felons' yard over the dividing wall, though visitors were charged 'footing', a fee which was used to provide the poorest with 'a more substantial meal than they were accustomed to enjoy'. Garnish existed but was used to buy a round of drinks for new inmates.

THE REFORMERS

Imprisonment as a punishment in itself really started to take hold during the hiatus between the end of transportation to America in the 1770s and the start of sending convicts to Australia in 1787. Something had to be done with these offenders and a spell in prison seemed the most expedient solution. By the turn of the century, with John Howard's research encouraging new ideas, people were also starting to question the whole penal system and wondering whether execution, flogging and the pillory were really appropriate in this more enlightened age.

Two people picked up the baton dropped when John Howard died in 1790; Elizabeth Fry, whose work in nineteenth century with female prisoners led directly to a spate of reforms across the entire prison system, and Jeremy Bentham, who freely acknowledged Howard's influence on his thinking. And were they led, others soon followed.

Elizabeth Fry (née Gurney) was born on 21 May 1780 into a prominent Norfolk Quaker banking family. Her mother died when she was twelve and she was partly responsible for bringing up her siblings including her brother John, who would later join her campaign for prison reform, and her sister Hannah, who married the prison reformer and anti-slavery campaigner Thomas Fowell Buxton. When Elizabeth was eighteen, she married a banker and fellow Quaker, Joseph Fry. They lived in London and had eleven children, only one of whom failed to survive into adulthood. Through her faith and family, she was connected to some of the most influential people in the country, including in banking, the Lloyds and the Barclays; in business, the Cadburys, the Rowntrees and the Frys; and, in politics, William Wilberforce.

She was a well-known minister and in keeping with her faith she worked among the poor and the sick including prisoners. 'I love to feel for the sorrows of others,' she wrote in 1797. Her first visit to Newgate was in 1812 when, entering the women's quarters against the advice of the keeper she was appalled at the filthy overcrowded conditions and the ragged violent women, some of whom were dressed in men's clothes as they had nothing else to wear. Two women were taking clothes from a dead baby to give to another child. There were fourteen prisoners aged 9-13 as well as the babies and children of the inmates. 'All I tell thee,' she told a fellow Quaker, 'is a faint picture of reality; the filth, the closeness of the rooms, the furious manner and expressions of the women towards each other, and the abandoned wickedness, which everything bespoke are really indescribable.' Later she told a parliamentary committee, 'We were witness to the dreadful proceedings that went forward on the female side of the prison; the begging, swearing, gaming, fighting, singing, dancing, dressing up in men's clothes.'

Although she returned the next day with food and clothes, family matters kept her away for four years. When she did return however it was the start of a revolution in the penal system. In 1817, she set up the Association for the Reform of Female Prisoners in Newgate as well as a school for the children. Almost immediately, she was besieged with requests from the women 'who earnestly entreated to be allowed to share in their instruction', sadly, though, due to lack of space she was obliged to refuse. But as the school flourished, she was able to include the mothers and teach them the Bible, temperance and hard work. A thief called Mary Connor was chosen by the other prisoners to be the teacher and classes included sewing and other skills that would make them employable on release. That same year, Fry was also successful in stopping the public flogging of women, though it continued in private until 1820. It was abolished for men, except in certain cases, in 1948. The last prison flogging in this country was in 1962.

The transformation was remarkable. The keeper, who had previous regarded the women as beyond hope, was encouraged to appoint a matron to supervise the cleanliness and tidiness of the ward. She was assisted by monitors chosen from among the prisoners by themselves. In a deal struck by Mrs Fry, the clothes the women made were sold to Richard Dixon and Co., which had the contract for supplying the convicts at Botany Bay in Australia. The regular money this brought in paid for 'small extra indulgences'.

Mrs Fry was very keen that other people, particularly women, should also visit the prisoners and they did. One who came was the Lord Mayor, who was so mightily impressed by the 'stillness and propriety' which had replaced the swearing, yelling catfights of before that he agreed that the City Corporation would pay some of the costs of the matron and the school. In 1819, the American ambassador praised her work and the philanthropist Robert Owen wrote to the papers praising Mrs Fry's and encouraging others to follow her.

Not everyone though thought she was a ministering angel. 'We long to burn her alive,' wrote the Reverend Sydney Smith waspishly in 1821. 'Examples of living virtue disturb our repose and give birth to distressing comparisons.'

As a result of Mrs Fry's evidence to parliament, the Home Secretary Robert Peel's Gaols Act of 1823 allowed that female prisoners should be guarded by female officers. In 1828, Mrs Fry's husband was declared bankrupt and her brother stepped in to finance her philanthropy, which had by now expanded beyond Newgate to prisons up and down the country.

In 1835 she was before a House of Lords committee recommending the complete segregation of male and female prisoners; the further division of female prisoners according to their crimes and criminal records into four groups distinguished in Newgate by different uniforms and badges. She also asked for better food, and that there should be no hard labour for women. However, despite her opposition to it, the Silent System was adopted in the new Prisons Act, 1835.

When she died in 1845 over a thousand people attended her burial in Barking.

Jeremy Bentham was a philosopher and jurist who founded the doctrine of utilitarianism under the guiding principle of 'it is the greatest happiness of the greatest number that is the measure of right and wrong' that still underpins much of our thinking today. He acknowledged a debt to John Howard's ideas on prison reform, which he heartily espoused. He believed in the isolation of prisoners to reflect on their sins and the benefits of work for prisoners, though the gruelling hard labour Bentham imposed may not have been quite what the more compassionate Howard had in mind.

Bentham was born in Spitalfields on 15 February 1748, the son of a wealthy lawyer who hoped his super-intelligent young son would follow him into the law. Instead, he chose to campaign for reform, not just of the legal system but in wider society. Some of his ideas such as the abolition of slavery and the abolition of the death penalty were in the vanguard of thinking for their time. Others, the legalisation of homosexuality, the equality of the sexes, universal suffrage and animal rights were downright revolutionary. But he did not get everything right, ideas such as the codification of the English Common Law, which he deemed a 'Demon of Chicane', were, and still are, rejected. And he corresponded with some of the most influential thinkers of his age including the philosopher and political economist Adam Smith and the French revolutionary aristocrat Mirabeau. The political economist, philosopher and feminist John Stuart Mill was a pupil.

His two major contributions to penal reform were the panopticon and the idea that prisoners should suffer a severe regime, as long as it wasn't detrimental to their health.

Bentham was incensed that the panopticon was rejected and he didn't take rejection well. The theory he developed as a result was based on the idea that there is a powerful elite conspiring to look after their own interests against those of the wider public. And it does not come as surprise to learn that he was for transparency and surveillance, which he saw as improving people's lives.

He died in June 1832 and his body, in accordance with his will was dissected, preserved, stuffed with straw and dressed in his clothes. It is on display at University College London, which he founded, where the head was eventually removed for safe-keeping and replaced by a dummy, after featuring in one too many student pranks.

REFORMS TO PUNISHMENTS

As the nineteenth century progressed and the penal system slowly ground its way to reform, so the use of the death penalty gradually declined, to be replaced by transportation. Hanging was, not surprisingly, still popular in the first twenty years of the century, averaging around eight to ten deaths in the first ten years and reaching a peak of forty-three in 1820.

In 1807, twenty-eight people were crushed to death when a pie seller's stall overturned and after this a secret underground tunnel was dug between St Sepulchre's and Newgate so the chaplain did not get held up and jostled by the mob trying to reach the condemned on a hanging day. Among the expectant crowd were always a large number of habitual criminals, either working or seeing off their friends. A nineteenth century governor of Newgate acknowledged that he'd never known a murderer who hadn't previously been at an execution.

From the beginning of the century, a small but vocal opposition to the death penalty had been forming as people began to question its effectiveness as a deterrent. This group was not united; some argued for the end of the capital punishment altogether, while others wanted it to be less of a public spectacle, or were in favour of more humane methods of execution. Others still wanted it to remain on the statue books as a threat but never carried out. From 1830, the abolitionists had the press on their side.

In 1843, Charles Dickens and William Thackeray were both at the hanging of François Courvoisier for killing his employer Lord William Russell (whose ancestor William Lord Russell had been executed in 1683 for his involvement in the Rye House Plot). Dickens, who was attending in an official capacity as a journalist, had rented a balcony to get a good view. Thackeray was there with a friend who was hoping the spectacle would persuade the writer to join the campaign to abolish the death penalty.

Thackeray arrived four hours early to find a large enthusiastic crowd had already gathered. By 6am, the street around the scaffold was full with around 40,000 people young and old, some sober, many drunk. There were families who had brought a picnic breakfast and celebrities, including Prince Augustus Frederick, Duke of Suffolk, son of George III to spot, as well as prostitutes to befriend. Up in the windows and balconies were the 600 ticket holders, including Dickens, who had paid up to £10 per person for a better seat. At 8am, Courvoisier was brought out, the noose placed round his neck and a hood over his eyes. Within minutes it was all over.

Afterwards Thackeray wrote, in his essay *On going to see a man hanged,* 'I feel myself shamed and degraded at the brutal curiosity that took me to that spot.' Recalling the event six years later in the *Daily News*, Dickens, always a man of many words, went into more detail. 'I did not see one token in all the immense crowd of any one emotion suitable to the occasion, nothing but ribaldry, levity, drunkenness, and flaunting vice in fifty other shapes.'

In 1868, hangings were moved inside Newgate where they continued in private until the prison closed. Dead Man's Walk, a long corridor of arches, led from the condemned cells to the gallows and a black flag was hoisted over the prison after an execution. The last person publicly hanged in England was a Fenian called Michael Barrett who had been convicted for his part in the Clerkenwell Explosion. This was an attempt to break one of his comrades out of Clerkenwell Prison using a bomb which had killed twelve people, injured 120 and damaged local houses but failed to free a single man. Barrett, despite declaring his innocence, was publicly hanged on 26 May 1868, just three days before hangings were moved inside Newgate. His execution drew an apathetic crowd just a few thousand strong.

He 'did not seem to struggle much,' said one witness dispassionately. 'His body swung round once or twice and then it was all over.'

There were refinements too to the hanging process. Originally in the Middle Ages with no other method or skills to hand, hangmen had used the short drop method, in which the condemned were pushed off a cart with noose round their necks. Death, which took between ten and twenty minutes, was by strangulation though if the hangman was merciful he would speed this up by hanging on the legs of the dying. A trapdoor method was introduced in 1783 when the execution site moved from Tyburn to Newgate, but death was still by strangulation.

The standard drop was introduced in 1866 when an Irishman, William Haughton, calculated that a drop of four to six feet (1.2-1.8m) would be enough to break a victim's neck. Since it broke the neck instantly thereby reducing suffering, it was considered more humane than the short drop. It couldn't always be guaranteed to work however, meaning the victim was still strangled. Sometimes, it worked too well and he or she was decapitated.

The long drop was the method used from 1872, when it was introduced by the hangman William Marwood, until the death penalty was abolished in 1965. It was an improvement to the standard drop since it took the condemned person's height and weight into account when calculating how much rope would be needed to effect a drop that guaranteed the neck would be broken every time - without decapitation. Careful positioning of the knot on the noose ensured the neck would break.

The effect of moving the executions inside Newgate, thereby hiding them from public view was to make them, as Henry Fielding had suggested a hundred years earlier, more terrible and more sinister. Nevertheless, crowds still gathered outside on the morning of a hanging to see the black flag raised to confirm a death. Public executions were banned in 1868, but the campaigners for total abolition still had many hurdles to overcome and it would be another century before that was achieved.

Although sodomy had been a capital offence for around 400 years, punishment had generally been in the pillory. However, at the end of the eighteenth century and in the early nineteenth century, there were a spate of convictions which changed things.

In 1811, an outraged and hostile crowd and several dandyish-looking gentlemen looked on as two soldiers were hanged for sodomy but convictions were rare, due to a lack of witnesses. The last men to be hanged for the offence were James Pratt and John Smith on 27 November 1835 - a decade that was a pivotal point in English penal reform. Sodomy carried the death penalty until 1861, but even after that the penalties were harsh. In 1885 any act of 'gross indecency' between men whether in public or in private was punishable with hard labour, as the playwright Oscar Wilde discovered to his cost.

The punishment of six men from the Vere St Coterie in the pillory for homosexual offences on 27 September 1810 marked the beginning of the end of the pillory. After this incident, its use declined and in 1815 it was restricted to perjurers. The last pillorying was in 1830 and it was finally abolished in 1837. The stocks followed in 1872. The last person to be pilloried in England was Peter James Bossy who was convicted of 'wilful and corrupt perjury' in 1830. He was offered the choice of seven years transportation or one hour in the pillory, and chose the latter.

Another popular and well-attended public event was whipping. Elizabeth Fry had managed to get the whipping of women and girls banned in public in 1817 and in private in 1820, but the public whipping at the cart's tail of men and boys was not stopped until the 1830s and it went on in private until 1948. Even some of those in the system were pleased when it ended; George Laval Chesteron, the governor of a house of correction in Clerkenwell, for one 'heartily rejoiced'.

Penal servitude was introduced by two acts in 1853 and 1857 and replaced transportation in cases where the sentence was less than fourteen years. After this, transportation fell into decline as a punishment. The last convict ship arrived in Australia in 1868.

For the most part, penal servitude included tedious activities such as picking oakum and breaking rocks. However, where the prisoner was skilled, or the local economy demanded it, there was the option of more useful employment such as making herring nets, shoemaking, tailoring or joinery. It was hard relentless and cruel and, because of the Silent System, carried out without communication with other prisoners, though they were irrepressible and non-verbal systems of communication soon developed. It was abolished in 1948.

In addition to the day-to-day work there was also hard labour as a form of punishment including the Treadmill a large paddle wheel on which a prisoner, male or female, would climb between 5,000 and 14,000feet for up to six hours a day. Shot Drill was simply moving cannonballs from one pile to another in the following prescribed method: stooping without bending the knees; lifting the cannonball to chest height; taking three steps to the right; placing it on the ground, again without bending the knees; stepping back three paces and repeating. It served no useful purpose and again this was for men and women. The crank machine was for men only. A handle turned a wheel and forced four large cups through sand in a drum. The prisoner had to turn the handle 14,000 times in a day (this was registered on a dial) and sometimes the warders would tighten the screw in the handle making the job harder.

Transportation to Australia began in 1787 when the first convict ships sailed from Portsmouth. In total, eleven ships set sail, that year of which six were convict ships carrying 775 convicts; the other five carried officials, crew, their families and children, numbering 645. The fleet arrived at Botany Bay (now part of Sydney) in January 1788 and established the first settlement.

Initially, there were a high number of deaths due to shortages of food, disease and the struggle to be self-sufficient; and conditions for the convicts were harsh and cruel with regular floggings with limitless lashes. In the 1830s and 1840s, there were efforts by the Lieutenant-General Sir Richard Bourke to limit the worst excesses, though these were vigorously resisted by those guarding the convicts. Because of the terror of being so far from home and the increasing opposition to capital punishment, it began to take over from the death penalty as the severest form of punishment in a large number of offences, particularly petty crime. By removing them from their sphere of influence, it also became a useful way of punishing political prisoners. Major crimes such as murder and rape were not transportable offences. After serving their sentence, many convicts stayed on to build new lives, and in time non-convicts emigrated to join this burgeoning new society. Ironically, one of the arguments behind stopping transportation was a reluctance on the part of the government to pay to send convicts to Australia, when fine upstanding citizens had to fund their own passage.

Ultimately, though, the system ended because it was expensive to run and the convicts were kept in appalling conditions. After 1840 it fell into decline. The Penal Servitude Act of 1857, which allowed the courts to impose a sentence of penal servitude instead of transportation, drove a further nail into its coffin. Transportation ended in 1868. Between 1787 and 1864 about 160,000 convicts were sent to Australia.

THE EXECUTIONERS

William Calcraft (1800-1879) served as public and private executioner for forty-five years from 1829-1874. According to a pamphlet published in 1846, *The Groans of the Gallows: of the Past and Present Life of William Calcraft, the Living Hangman of Newgate*, he was the orphan son of a farmer and a cobbler by trade who had a sideline selling pies at executions. It is through this that he is thought to have got the job as executioner.

In addition to a retainer of 25s a week, he received a guinea for each hanging at Newgate and half a crown for a flogging. The superstition that the hanged could cure illnesses, and were therefore lucky, still held true so, in addition to this, there was extra money to be made selling inch lengths of the hangman's rope, for as much as 5s an inch if the condemned man had been famous. By now Mme Tussaud was in town and making wax models of the most celebrated criminals. Calcraft flogged her their clothes and other effects so she could dress her effigies authentically, so it appears the dead were lucky at least for him. He also charged other gaols around the country £10 or more to come and execute their inmates. He was an advocate of the short drop method and it is estimated that in a forty-five-year career he executed 450 people nationally.

William Marwood, who took over from Calcraft, was also a cobbler. He came late to the role of executioner, performing his first hanging at Lincoln Castle Gaol in 1872 at the age of 54. The efficient way he dispatched William Frederick Horry led to his appointment as the executioner at Newgate. He received a salary of £20 a year plus £10 per execution. Marwood's revolutionary technique was the long drop, which broke the prisoner's neck instantly, an improvement on the distressing short drop method of the past. In his nine years as hangman, Marwood executed 176 people nationally. Along with Jack Ketch, he was one of only two executioners to give their name to the hangman character in Punch and Judy. And in his day there was a popular rhyme that went:

'If Pa killed Ma
Who'd kill Pa?
Marwood.'

James Berry was a Yorkshireman, former police officer and friend of Marwood, who favoured and refined the long drop method and loved a good story, especially if he was telling it. He worked as an executioner from 1884 to 1891 when hangings were in private, and could be found holding court in the pub on the night before regaling the bar with tales of his executions. He executed 131 people nationally, including five women and William Bury, one of the men suspected of being Jack the Ripper, though two of his executions resulted in near or total decapitations. In 1885 he was the executioner at the hanging of John 'Babbacombe' Lee, 'the man they couldn't hang' where the trapdoor failed three times to open. Eventually, Lee's sentence was commuted to life imprisonment.

THE FINAL DAYS

In reality, Newgate was too small and old-fashioned to adapt properly to the new thinking. This became increasingly apparent after 1877 when the Home Office took it over, and it began to fall into decline. Transportation had ceased in 1868 and the death penalty was barely used in comparison with a hundred years earlier. Women were now more likely to be sent to Holloway and in 1869 the Debtors' Act reduced the power of the courts to sentence debtors to prison. From then until the end of the century Newgate was in serious decline. In 1902 it closed and the last surviving inmates were sent to Pentonville and Holloway. The scaffold too went to Pentonville. An auction was held at the prison on 4 February 1903 to sell off relics but, despite the enthusiastic efforts of a jolly auctioneer, the 214 lots made a paltry £980. Madame Tussaud's, which over the years had taken so many of the condemned prisoners' effects for their Chamber of Horrors, paid £100 for the bell that had tolled away the hours before an execution. Newgate was demolished between 1902 and 1904 and the Central Criminal Court of the Old Bailey now occupies the site.

Two pieces of Newgate remain in the City: part of the wall is in Amen Corner a private close off Warwick Lane owned by St Paul's Cathedral, and a door from the prison is in the Museum of London.

NEWGATE'S INMATES

Three cases from the nineteenth century demonstrate the attitude of the mob and involve a disgraced soldier, a group of gay men and a failed plot to overthrow the government.

Joseph Wall

Joseph Wall was made Lieutenant-Governor of Gorée a slave-trading island off Senegal in 1779 after a military career that was, at times distinguished and at others blighted by allegations of cruelty. On the voyage out to the island he had a convict flogged so harshly that he died. Gorée was a hot, filthy, disease-ridden backwater; after three years Wall's health was failing and he was making plans to come home.

In July, shortly before he was due to leave, he was approached by a deputation from the army asking for back pay owing in their wages. Wall, who was drunk, had the leader Sergeant Benjamin Armstrong and seven men arrested on a charge of mutiny. The next day and without holding a court martial, he had them all flogged with the men receiving between forty-seven and 800 lashes. Three of them, including Armstrong, died.

Back in England, one of Wall's former officers, Captain Roberts brought charges of cruelty against him. However, when the ship bringing other witnesses was reported lost, the charges were dropped. Wall retired to Somerset but his luck was running out. The ship might have been lost but some of the witnesses were not. When they arrived back in London, a warrant was issued for Wall's arrest, but he escaped while being brought to London to face trial and skipped to the continent where he lived quietly for a number of years under a false name, even enjoying the occasional trip back to England.

In October 1801, he wrote to the Home Secretary Lord Pelham offering to stand trial. He was arrested shortly after and charged with the murder of the three soldiers Gorée. On 20 January, he was tried in a session that lasted from 9am to 11pm and found guilty of the murder of Sgt. Armstrong. After eight days of appeals he was taken from the condemned cell at Newgate prison and hanged in front of a cheering crowd appalled at his cruelty.

A Mr J.T. Smith, who'd pulled strings with the ordinary Dr Ford, was allowed to meet him before he died. He wrote:

'As we crossed the press-yard a cock crew, and the solitary clanking of a restless chain was dreadfully horrible. The prisoners had not risen. Upon our entering a cold stone room, a most sickly stench of green twigs, with which an old round-shouldered, goggle-eyed man was endeavouring to kindle a fire, annoyed me almost as much as the canister fumigation of the doctor's Hatton Garden friends.

'The prisoner entered. He was death's counterfeit, tall, shrivelled, and pale; and his soul shot so piercingly through the port-holes of his head, that the first glance of him nearly terrified me. I said in my heart, putting my pencil in my pocket, "God forbid that I should disturb thy last moments!" His hands were clasped, and he was truly penitent. After the yeoman had requested him to stand up, he "pinioned him", as the Newgate phrase is, and tied the cord with so little feeling, that the governor, who had not given the wretch the accustomed fee, observed, "You have tied me very tight", upon which Dr. Ford ordered him to slacken the cord, which he did, but not without muttering. "Thank you, sir," said the governor to the doctor, "it is of little moment." He then observed to the attendant, who had brought in an immense iron shovelful of coals to throw on the fire, "Ay, in one hour that will be a blazing fire," then, turning to the doctor, questioned him, "Do tell me, sir: I am informed I shall go down with great force; is that so?" After the construction and action of the machine had been explained the doctor questioned the governor as to what kind of men he had at Goree. "Sir," he answered, "they sent me the very riff-raff." The poor soul then joined the doctor in prayer; and never did I witness more contrition at any condemned sermon than he then evinced.'

On the way home, Mr Smith ran across the hangman who was selling the rope that had hanged Governor Wall for a shilling an inch, an old man with an identical rope, who was undercutting him to the tune of sixpence an inch and, a bit further on at the corner of Newgate Street and Warwick Lane, a woman doing the same thing.

The Vere Street Coterie

In 1810, six men were pilloried after being convicted of 'unnatural offences' following a raid on the White Swan, a molly house (gay club) on Vere Street, off Oxford Street. When the procession left Newgate bound for the pillory, hostile crowds lined the streets armed with missiles and carts piled high with offal, dung, rotting fish, guts and rotten vegetables were waiting at the site on Haymarket. The men were 'protected' by two hundred police, a hundred on foot and a hundred armed and mounted. If the beaten-up prisoners had resembled 'bears dipped in a stagnant pool' when they left Newgate, within no time the cart was filled with the rotten vegetables and dead cats thrown by the hostile crowd and the six men were scarcely recognisable as human beings.

Once the first four, Philip Islet, William Thompson, Richard Francis and James Done, been put in the pillory, 'upwards of fifty women were permitted to stand in the ring, who assailed them with mud, dead cats, rotten eggs, potatoes, of buckets filled with blood, offal and dung'. When their hour was up it was the turn of the White Swan's landlord, James Cooke, and William Amos, also known as Sally Fox, who had a previous conviction, to receive the same appalling treatment. They suffered worse than the first four and Cooke was beaten almost insensible.

The next day the newspaper the *Morning Chronicle* called for a change in the law - not to ban the pillory itself which it considered no deterrent, but because 'it is horrible to accustome [sic] the people to take the vengeance of justice into their own hands'. Squeamishly, the paper declined to debate the issue of homosexuality, blaming it on war and foreigners.

The Cato Street Conspiracy

The Cato Street Conspiracy was a plot to murder the British cabinet and the Prime Minister in 1820 by a group of radical revolutionaries enraged by the Peterloo Massacre. However, the leader Arthur Thistlewood was unaware that his deputy George Edwards was a police spy.

On 22 February, Edwards, in a move that today would look suspiciously like entrapment, suggested they could take advantage of the political problems in the country to overthrow the government. He even provided funds to help arm the conspirators. The plan was to kill the politicians while they were at a dinner, seize key buildings, overthrow the government and oversee a revolution.

Thistlewood loved the idea. He thought it would trigger a massive popular uprising and evidently, over the next few hours, twenty-seven men thought so too and joined the plot. The conspirators rented a small house in Cato St as their headquarters. Meanwhile, Edwards was keeping the Home Office informed and they duly publicised the time and date of a fictitious dinner. The plan nearly went awry when one of the conspirators, the black political activist William Davidson, went to the venue for the event but failed to get any more information on it. In spite of this Thistlewood was determined to press ahead immediately.

But the Bow Street magistrate and twelve of his Bow Street Runners were on the case. The next evening, they stormed the house in Cato Street, determined to arrest the conspirators. In the ensuing brawl Thistlewood killed a runner with a sword, while others resisted arrest. Some went quietly. Davidson was arrested but Thistlewood and three others escaped through a back window. They were arrested a few days later.

At the trial five of the conspirators were sentenced to transportation and five, including Thistlewood and Davidson, to hanging and beheading. A crowd of thousands, some having paid three guineas to secure a good spot, saw them die on 1 May 1820. Infantry, two troops of Life Guards and eight pieces of artillery were stationed nearby in case of trouble, but the crowd was very well-behaved. After the men were dead they were cut down and beheaded, the severed heads held up for the crowd to boo and hiss, until one was dropped and they shouted 'Butterfingers!'.

Famous Newgate Prisoners

ROBIN HOOD - outlaw

It has been suggested that the legendary outlaw Robin Hood might have been based on the thirteenth century outlaw called Roger Godberd. Godberd served under Simon de Montfort, the sixth Earl of Leicester, who deposed Henry III, in a rebellion between 1263 and 1264 and became the de facto ruler of England. De Montfort was, in turn, deposed and killed in 1265 at the Battle of Evesham. Two centuries later it was claimed by the Scottish chronicler Walter Bower, that Godberd became an outlaw as a result of this defeat.

In 1267, he was living in Sherwood Forest and could call upon the support of 100 men. In 1272, he was captured by the Sheriff of Nottingham, but managed to escape. Eventually, he was recaptured and over the next three years was kept in three different prisons. His trial took place at the Tower and one source says that he died in Newgate in 1276, though another suggests that he lived out his old age on his farm.

BEN JONSON - playwright

Ben Jonson (1572-1637) made his name during the reign of James 1 writing satirical plays including *Volpone* and *The Alchemist*. His importance to English drama is seen as second only to Shakespeare.

In 1597, *The Isle of Dogs*, a play he co-wrote with Thomas Nashe, caused great offence and was banned. While Nashe escaped to Great Yarmouth, Jonson was arrested and sent to the Marshalsea for 'leude and mutynous behaviour' along with two of the actors Gabriel Spenser and Robert Shaw, but they were later released. A year later, Jonson killed Spenser in a duel and was sent to Newgate to await trial. Despite not being in religious orders, he pleaded benefit of the clergy and got off, though he was branded on the thumb to stop him using it again.

MARY FRITH aka MOLL CUTPURSE - notorious pickpocket and fence

Wild child Mary Frith came to be known as Moll Cutpurse from her 'career' as a thief. She also gained a reputation as a fence and a pimp. She was born in the 1580s and was out-of-control even as a child. She grew up to scandalise London by preferring men's clothes, dressing in a doublet and breeches, smoking a pipe and swearing. She was branded on the hand four times for theft and was sentenced to stand in a sheet outside St Paul's as a punishment for wearing men's clothes. It didn't stop her. She was incredibly vain and her home was stocked with mirrors so she could check her reflection. It was immaculate and feminine and she loved her dogs, mastiffs, which had their own beds with sheets and blankets.

She married in 1614, but professed to be uninterested in sex. By the 1620s she was working as a fence and a pimp procuring young women for men and male lovers for wives. She was sent to Bedlam but released in 1644 after apparently been cured of insanity. She is reputed to have shot General Fairfax, the Parliamentary Commander-in-Chief during the Civil War, in the arm and that to escape Newgate and the gallows she paid a bribe of £2,000. She died of dropsy on 26 July 1659.

JOHN COOK - prosecutor of Charles I and regicide

John Cook was the Solicitor-General under Oliver Cromwell's Commonwealth who led the prosecution of Charles I. He also advocated many reforms that were way ahead of his time, including a prisoner's right to silence; the cab-rank rule of advocacy - under which a barrister cannot pick and choose his cases, but is obliged to take the next appropriate one that comes along; abolition of imprisonment for debt and restrictions on the use of the death penalty.

When Charles I refused to recognise the legality of the court convened to try him, or to answer the charges of tyranny and high treason against him, Cook accepted to lead the prosecution.

At the Restoration, the Indemnity and Oblivion Act exempted the majority of the monarchy's opponents from prosecution for crimes committed during the Civil War and the Interregnum. Regicides, however, were not exempted. Cook was seized and imprisoned. Though he conducted his own defence at his trial, Cook was convicted of high treason and was hanged, drawn and quartered on 16 October 1660.

WILLIAM KIDD - pirate and privateer

Scotsman William Kidd (1645-1701) was based in New York and operated in the Caribbean, looting French ships between 1689 and 1695 when he was asked by the Earl of Bellomont, the British governor of New York, to attack known pirates and as well as the French. The venture was funded by Bellomont and four of the wealthiest men in England, all Whigs, and endorsed by William III, who stood to receive ten per cent of any booty. It established Kidd's reputation as a pirate, which by 1698 was so notorious for cruelty and torture that the Royal Navy was ordered to seize him. After a mutiny in which most of his sailors joined rival ships, he sailed home to New York via the Caribbean, hiding treasure on the way and learning that he was wanted both by the British navy and his mutinous crew.

Bellomont, realising the only way to save his own neck was to give up Kidd, had him arrested and sent to London to be questioned. There, the Tory government hoped to use him to discredit his wealthy Whig backers, but Kidd stayed loyal, trusting that they would intercede on his behalf. When they didn't, Kidd was sent to Newgate to await trial for murder and five counts of piracy on the high seas.

He was found guilty and hanged on 23 May 1701 at Execution Dock in Wapping. The rope broke on the first attempt and the process was repeated. His body hung in a gibbet for three years over the Thames at Tilbury as a warning to other would-be pirates.

GIACOMO CASANOVA - adventurer and author

Venetian Giacomo Casanova (1725-1798) is better known as a libertine than for his other pursuits as a writer, a spy or an occultist. In the eighteenth century, he charmed, gambled and intrigued his way round Europe, womanising and getting into trouble for outrages against religion. He was briefly in Newgate, allegedly for bigamy.

JAMES MACLAINE - the 'Gentleman Highwayman'

After squandering his inheritance on fashionable clothes, gambling and prostitutes, MacLaine moved from Dublin, where he grew up, to London where he married, and set himself up as a grocer. Following the death of his wife, MacLaine ruined the business chasing after wealthy women in the hope one would marry him. None did, so in 1750 he turned to highway robbery with his accomplice, a failed apothecary called William Plunkett. They operated in Hyde Park, then a relative wilderness and over six months carried out twenty hold-ups, including the Whig politician and man of letters, Horace Walpole, during which time they garnered a reputation for courtesy and restraint. Maclaine was arrested after the stolen goods he was selling were recognised and the constable was called.

Many fashionable people turned out to see the spectacle of his trial at the Old Bailey and it is said he received round 3,000 visitors while in Newgate. He was convicted and though his clergyman brother travelled from the Netherlands to plead for clemency, MacLaine was hanged at Tyburn on 3 October 1750.

MARY WADE - youngest female convict transported to Australia

Mary Wade was 11 years old when she was transported to Australia in 1789. She had been sentenced to hanging for stealing a cotton frock, a linen tippet and a linen cap from an eight-year-old girl who was collecting water in a bottle at a privy. She was reported by another child. On 11 March 1789, a proclamation was issued announcing that the king, George III had been cured of his unnamed madness and five days later, all the women on death row, including Mary, had their sentences commuted to penal transportation. By the time her convict ship, the *Lady Juliana* sailed, she had spent ninety-three days in Newgate. The ship, which was the first to carry only women and children, took eleven months to reach Sydney arriving on 3 June 1790. From there Mary was sent to Norfolk Island, a tiny island east of Sydney between New Caledonia and New Zealand. She arrived on 7 August 1790 and lived there for thirteen years during which time she had three children. Returning to Australia, she lived near the Hawkesbury River, north of Sydney and raised a family of twenty-one children, seven of whom lived to have children of their own. After some further setbacks, the family thrived and when Mary died on 17 December 1859 aged 82, hers was the first funeral service to be held in a church built on land donated by her son. When she died she had over 300 descendants.

CATHERINE WILSON (1822-20 October 1862)

Catherine Wilson worked as a nurse in Lincolnshire and Cumbria and was married to a man named Dixon. When Dixon died, shortly after the wedding, a bottle of colchicum was found in his room, Wilson begged the doctor not to perform a post mortem and he backed down.

By 1862, Wilson was working as a live-in nurse to Mrs Sarah Canell, who died after drinking sulphuric acid given to her by Wilson. At her trial, Wilson claimed the pharmacist had given her the acid in error. To the incredulity of the judge, she was acquitted. However, Wilson was rearrested on leaving court charged with the murder of seven other patients. This time the authorities were playing it safe and she was tried on only one count: the murder of Mrs Maria Soames in 1856.

At the trial it was alleged that seven of her employers had written wills in her favour before they died, but the evidence was not admitted. Nevertheless, she was found guilty and sentenced to death. Twenty thousand people turned up to see her hang outside Newgate on 20 October 1862. She was the last woman to be publicly hanged in London. Speaking in private afterwards, the judge, Mr Justice Byles, congratulated her defence counsel on his skilful handling of her case calling Wilson 'the greatest criminal that ever lived'.

APPENDIX 2
NEWGATE IN CULTURE

Newgate has featured in art and literature almost since the day it was built. Here is a brief list of some works it has inspired.

1386-9 - *The Canterbury Tales*, **Geoffrey Chaucer**

Perkin Reveller and his friends in The Cook's Tale sometimes find themselves in Newgate after one too many.

1722 - *Moll Flanders*, **Daniel Defoe**

In Moll Flanders, the heroine Moll is born in Newgate after her mother pleads the belly and wins a reprieve. When her mother is transported to America, Moll is raised by a foster mother.

1728 - *The Beggar's Opera*, **John Gay**

A ballad opera in three acts set in Newgate. Some of the characters are supposedly based on real people, for example, Peachum the thief-taker was based on Jonathan Wild and the robber Macheath on Jack Sheppard. The whole was intended to satirise the government of Prime Minister Robert Walpole with Walpole cast as Macheath. It was an instant hit, running for ninety nights when it opened at Lincoln's Inn Fields in 1728. *The Craftsman*, the leading opposition newspaper of the day, said it had opened to great applause and would probably 'make the Rich very Gay and Gay very Rich'. However, within two weeks the paper had changed its tune publishing an article denouncing the work as libellous. To the horror of moralists, magistrates and government supporters, it was frequently revived. Gay's sequel *Polly*, another political satire potentially more outspoken than *The Beggar's Opera* was suppressed by the Lord Chamberlain. It wasn't performed until fifty years later.

1762 - *The Adventures of Sir Launcelot Greaves*, **Tobias Smollett**

Smollett was imprisoned himself in at the King's Bench and fined £100. He drew on this for his novel *The Adventures of Sir Launcelot Greaves*, which was serialised in *The British Magazine* of which he was editor in 1760. In it the squire says, 'I've had an ugly dream, I thought, for all the world, they were carrying me to Newgate, and that there was Jack Ketch coom to vetch me before my taim'.

1820s-1840s *The Newgate Novels*

A controversial genre of novels, which drew their inspiration from the Newgate Calendar and were thought to glamorise the lives of criminals. Thackeray was a vociferous opponent and satirised them in his own writing. *Catherine*, which he wrote in 1839, was a satire of the genre though many missed the point and it was sometimes categorised as a Newgate novel itself.

1836 - *A Visit To Newgate*, Charles Dickens

In 1836, Dickens published his lengthy pen portrait of a visit to the gaol. Newgate features in four of his novels *Barnaby Rudge* (1841), *Oliver Twist* (1846), *A Tale Of Two Cities* (1859) and *Great Expectations* (1861).

1967 - *Smith*, Leon Garfield

The story of resourceful, uneducated Smith a pickpocket in an eighteenth century London underworld of criminals and hangmen that is dominated by Newgate prison.

1969 - Where's Jack?

Starring Tommy Steele as Jack Sheppard and Stanley Baker as Jonathan Wild this film covers the adventures and exploits of the notorious thief and prison-breaker.

1999 - *Plunkett and Macleane*, dir. Jake Scott

A film starring Robert Carlyle as Will Plunkett and Jonny Lee Miller as Macleane in a retelling of the highwaymen's story.

APPENDIX 3
NEWGATE CANT

Newgate Cant was the language of the inmates and a version of thieves' cant the language of highwaymen and other criminals. It was collected into books and the some of the words passed into everyday speech. Surviving examples include 'pulling one's leg', 'left in the lurch' and 'swell'.

A

Active citizen - a louse

Adam's Ale - water

Arch Duke, Dimber Damber Upright man - chief of a gang of thieves or gypsies

Arch Dell, Arch Doxy - chief of a gang of female canters or gypsies

Ard - hot

Autem-bawler – a parson

Autem Divers - Pickpockets who practice in churches, also churchwardens and overseers of the poor

Adam Tile - a pickpocket's assistant who runs off with the lifted goods

Aunt - Mine aunt, a bawd or procuress, a title of eminence for senior dells who serve as instructresses and midwives for the dells

B

Bawd - a procuress

Beater cases - boots

Belly cheat - an apron

Belly timber - food of all sorts

Ben - a fool

Bene - good, Benar better

Bene bowse - good beer or other strong liquor

Bene darkens - goodnight

Bene fearers - counterfeiters of bills

Beneshiply - worshipfully

Bilk - to cheat. Let us bilk the rattling cove; let us cheat the hackney coachman of his fare

Bing - to go. Bing avast - get you gone. Bing avast in a darkmans; stole away in the night.

Bingo - brandy or other spirits

Black art - the art of picking a lock

Black box - a lawyer

Blanket hornpipe - amorous congress

Bleating cheat - a sheep

Bleating rig - sheep stealing

Bluffer - an innkeeper

Blunt - money

Boung - a purse

Boung nipper - a cut purse. Formerly purses were worn at the girdle, from whence they were cut.

Bufe - a dog

Bufe nabber - a dog stealer

Bus-napper - a constable

Buzman - a pickpocket

C

Cackle - to blab or discover secrets. The cull is leaky and cackles - the rogue tells all

Cackling cheat - a hen

Cackling farts - eggs

Calle - cloak or gown

Captain Sharp - a cheating bully, or one in a set of gamblers, whose office is to bully any pigeon, who, suspecting roguery, refuses to pay what he has lost

Chive - a knife, file or saw

Cockles - to cry cockles, to be hanged: perhaps from the noise made while strangling

College - Newgate or any other prison. He has been educated at the steel and took his last degree at college; he has received his education at the house of correction and was hanged at Newgate

Colt - one who lets horses to highwaymen, also a boy newly initiated into roguery

Crack lay - house breaking

Cramp rings - bolts, shackles, fetters

Cramp words - the sentence of death passed on a criminal by a judge

Crank - the falling sickness

Counterfeit-crank - a genteel cheat, sham or imposter - sometimes a forger, impersonator, clipper or coiner, fake jewels merchant, fly-by-night. Also a beggar who pretends to be ill or injured to inspire greater pity

D

Dag - a gun
Darbies - irons. Fetters
Darkmans - the night
Deusaville - the countryside
Dew beaters - feet
Dews wins or Deux wins - tuppence
Drag lay - waiting in the streets to rob carts or wagons

E

Earth bath - a grave
Evil - a halter. Also a wife

F

Fams, Fambles - hands - famble cheats; rings or gloves
To fib - to beat. Fib the cove's quern in the rumpad for the lour in his
    bung; beat the fellow in the highway for the money in his purse.
Flash the hash - vomit
Fly - a wagon
Fog - smoke
Fog - tobacco. Tip me a gage of focus; give me a pipe of tobacco
Frummagemmed - Choked, strangled, suffocated or hanged

G

Gan - the mouth or the lips
Gape-seed - whatever a crowd idly gawps at - puppet shows, freaks,
    mountebanks etc
Glazier - one who breaks windows - glasses, to steal goods exposed for
    sale. Glaziers; eyes
Glimmer - fire
Glimstick - a candlestick
Go west - go to the gallows
Grog blossom - a carbuncle, or pimple on the face, caused by excessive
    drinking

H

Heave - to rob. To heave a case; to rob a house. To heave a bough; to rob
    a booth.
Heels - To be laid out by the heels, to be confined or put in prison
High pad - a highwayman
Hike - to hike off; to run away

Hog - a shilling

Hoker/Angler - a thief who robs houses through upper storey windows by
means of a pole with a hook on the end

The hums - a congregation

Hunting - drawing unwary persons to play or game

I

In the Newgate - in the middle pocket of a coat where the thieves can't
reach

J

Jack in a box - a Sharper or cheat. Also a child in its mother's womb

Jarkeman - a forger, especially the faker of licences to perform a trade, to
travel or to beg

Jammed - hanged

Jem - a gold ring

Jenny - an instrument for lifting up the grate or to of a show-glass in order
to rob it

Juggler's box - the engine for burning culprits in the hand

K

Ken - a house. A bob ken, or a bowman ken; a well-furnished house, also
a house that harbours thieves. Biting the ken; robbing the house

Kimbaw - to trick, cheat or cozen; also to beat or bully

King's Head Inn or Chequer Inn, in Newgate Street - the prison of
Newgate

Knot - a gang of villains

L

Lage - water

Lay - enterprise, pursuit or attempt: to be sick of the lay. It also means a
hazard or chance: he stands a queer lay; he is in danger

Lib - to lie together

Libbege - a bed

Lightens - the day

Lord of the Manor of Tyburn - the hangman

Low pad - a footpad

Lullaby cheat - an infant

M

Mad Tom or Mad Tom of Bedlam - otherwise an Abram man (i.e. naked).
    A rogue who counterfeits madness
Maunding - asking or begging
Melt - to spend. Will you melt a border? Will you spend a shilling?
Mish - a shirt, a smock, a sheet
Mort - a woman
Mow heater - a drover. From their frequent sleeping on hay mows

N

Napper of naps - a sheep stealer
Newgate bird - a thief, who frequently finds themselves caged in Newgate
Newgate fashion - two by two - how prisoners were marched off for
    transportation
Newgate frisk or hornpipe - dancing in the air - hanging
Newgate seize me! - a binding oath among criminals
Newgate solicitor - a pettyfogging and roguish attorney
Nubbing - hanging. The nubbing cheat; the gallows. The nubbing cove;
    the hangman. The nubbing ken; the sessions house

O

Old - ugly
Old toast - a brisk old fellow.
Olli Compolli - the name of one of the principal rogues of the canting
    crew
Oschives - bone-handled knives

P

Pike - to go
Pinked - pricked with a sword in a duel

Q

Quit - to set free, discharge

R

Rum - great
Rum-mort - a queen or great lady
Rum-padders - highwaymen

S

Skrip - a paper
Smoke - to suspect or smell a design as in 'He smoked it out'
Snaffle - to steal, rob, purloin. Thus a horse thief is a snaffler of prancers
Swell - great

T

Take a ride to Tyburn - attend your own hanging
Twig - to snap or break off, to disengage
Tyburn blossom - a young thief or pickpocket who will grow and ripen
    into fruit for the gallows. Someone born to be hanged
Tyburn tippet - the hangman's halter

W

Whip-jacks - the nineteenth order of the canting-crew - counterfeit sailors
    begging with false tales of shipwrecks, losses at sea, drowned
    children
Whit - Newgate itself

Extract from *1811 Dictionary of the Vulgar Tongue* by Francis Grose, published
as an ebook by Project Gutenberg

BIBLIOGRAPHY

BOOKS

BABINGTON: Anthony: *The English Bastille: A History of Newgate Gaol and Prison Conditions 1188-1902* (MacDonald & Co, 1971)

BRANDON, David, BROOKE, Alan: *Olde London Punishments* (The History Press, 2010)

DICKENS, Charles: *A Visit To Newgate, from Sketches by Boz* (John Macrone, 1860) British Library

GROVIER, Kelly: *The Gaol* (John Murray, 2008)

HALLIDAY, Stephen: *Newgate: London's Prototype Of Hell* (The History Press, 2007)

HITCHCOCK, Tim, SHOEMAKER, Robert: *Tales From The Hanging Court*, (Hodder Arnold, 2008)

HOWARD, John: *The State of the Prisons in England and Wales* (1777 & subsequent editions)

INGLIS, Lucy: *Georgian London: Into The Streets* (Viking, 2013)

MCCONVILLE, Sean: *A History of English Prison Administration* (Routledge & Kegan Paul, 1981)

PICARD, Liza: *Dr Johnson's London: Everyday Life in London in the Mid Eighteenth Century* (Orion, 2000)

RUMBELOW, Donald: *The Triple Tree* (Harrap, 1982)

VARIOUS AUTHORS: *The Scoundrels Dictionary* (Gale ECCO, Print Editions, 2010)

WHITE, Jerry: *London In The Eighteenth Century: A Great And Monstrous Thing* (Bodley Head, 2012)

WHITE, Jerry: *London In The Nineteenth Century: A Human Awful Wonder Of God* (Bodley Head, 2007)

ONLINE

The Chronicles of Newgate, Arthur George Frederick Griffiths (Chapman & Hall, 1884) https://books.google.co.uk/books

1811 Dictionary of the Vulgar Tongue, Francis Grose (Project Gutenberg, www.gutenberg.net)

www.encyclopaediabritannica.com

Howard League for Penal Reform Howardleague.org

The International Movie Database imdb.com

The National Archives www.nationalarchives.gov.uk
Newgate http://www.british-history.ac.uk/old-new-london/vol2/pp441-461
www.british-history.ac.uk/plea-memoranda-rolls/vol3/pp36-49#fnn13
oldbaileyonline.org
Prisons and Punishments in Late Medieval London, Christine
      Winter https://pure.royalholloway.ac.uk/portal/
      files/16684548/2013WinterCLPhD.pdf.pdf Christine Winter

Index